Feminism.
A Quick Immersion

Noëlle McAfee

FEMINISM
A Quick Immersion

Tibidabo Publishing
New York

Copyediting by Lori Gerson
Cover art by Raimon Guirado

First published 2021

Visit our Series on our Web:
www.quickimmersions.com

ISBN: 978-1-949845-26-6
1 2 3 4 5 6 7 8 9 10

Library of Congress Control Number: 2021933254

Printed in the United States of America.

Contents

.

Introduction

Sara Ahmed begins her book, *Living a Feminist Life*, with the words, "What do you hear when you hear the word *feminism*?" Ahmed tells us what she hears: "It is a word that fills me with hope, with energy. It brings to mind loud acts of refusal and rebellion as well as the quiet ways we might have of not holding on to things that diminish us. It brings to mind women who have stood up, spoken back, risked lives, homes, relationships in the struggle for more bearable worlds."

I share Ahmed's exuberance about what feminism offers. If only I had known about it as a child. Growing up in the 1960s, I didn't know there was such a thing as feminism, but I keenly felt the need for it. I was angry at all the commercials peddling cleaning products to women. Why couldn't a man do the laundry? I felt constricted by the help wanted ads that I came across reading the daily paper—I read everything—which were split between jobs for women and jobs for men. I was disheartened by the narrow range of professions open to women: nurse, teacher, secretary, occupations that all seemed to be geared toward taking care of someone else. I was happy that I scored poorly on the section of standardized exams designed to assess clerical ability. At least maybe I would not have to be a secretary! I never even considered possibilities like scientist, artist, professor, and certainly not philosopher. I could have hardly imagined that I would grow up to be a professor of philosophy at a world-renowned university and the author of five books and dozens of articles.

I learned about feminism as I was turning 17, when a friend invited me to go with her to the National Women's Conference being held in our home town, Houston, Texas. When we arrived, I did not recognize all the super stars of the feminist movement, but my friend pointed them out to me: There's Bella Abzug, Betty Friedan, Gloria Steinem! I did recognize Jean Stapleton, the actress who played Edith Bunker, the long-suffering wife of Archie Bunker, the famous bigot of the popular sitcom *All in the Family*. My friend and I walked around visiting various demonstrations on the Convention grounds, some calling for public funding of child care, others for lesbian rights, and others for reproductive freedom. It was strange to see Edith Bunker—no, Jean Stapleton—on the stage in the huge arena calling for equal rights for women and then the thousands of women in the room chanting in thunderous unison, "ERA Yes! ERA Yes! ERA Yes!" ERA stood for the then pending Equal Rights Amendment to the U.S. Constitution, which for the first time would specify equal rights for women, something until then absent in the nation's founding document. It stated simply, "Equality of rights under the law shall not be denied or abridged by the United States or by any state on account of sex."

When I returned to school the next day, I pasted an "ERA Yes" sticker on my locker. At the end of the day I returned to see that someone had angrily scratched it off. The ERA never passed and still there is no explicit mention of women or sex in the U.S. Constitution. Right there I became an advocate for women's rights, but a few years later in my twenties most of the women I knew disavowed feminism. It seemed to have for them connotations of militancy and man hating, when, after all, aren't we all equal now?

Now in the twenty-first century, most women would answer with a resounding "no" to the question of whether women are equal. Yes from a philosophical point of view they are equal, but from a daily, lived experience point of view, they are not. The #MeToo movement documents the way women are still preyed upon at work. One global crisis after another disproportionately harms women. Perhaps for a minute it felt like things were going well for women, but today most women know this is not the case. And now women and men are calling themselves feminists, even if many of them are not entirely sure what that means.

This Quick Immersion will visit many of feminism's moments of refusal and rebellion as well as the moments of women working for more bearable worlds. We will see that there isn't just one kind of feminism but a variety of feminist approaches and points of view; but all are trying to make sense of the problem that, for most of the past three millennia, if not longer, the world over women have been treated as the property of men, deprived of the ability to chart their own life, and subject to random acts of violence. Despite the considerable respect and legal rights that women have won over the past century, women are still vulnerable. According to the World Health Organization, one in three women have experienced physical and/or sexual violence. Throughout the world, women are paid less than men for equal work and more likely to live in poverty. In many parts of the world, women still lack basic civil and political rights. According to the Global Fund for Women, "214 million women worldwide want, but lack access to, contraception; more than 800 women die daily from preventable causes related to pregnancy and childbirth; and same-sex relationships between consenting adults are still illegal in 76 countries globally." Mothers teach their daughters how to "behave" in a way to keep them safe, at the same time both protecting their daughters from the inequities of a sexist society and perpetuating the expectations that keep them in place. Even in the developed world, women's hold on newfound rights is still tenuous. Professional women still find themselves doing the bulk of cooking, cleaning, and child care. And in most any place in the world, even the most developed, women hesitate to walk down a dark street alone.

How is it that, in the twenty-first century, these inequities continue? And why is it that they are more or less generally accepted as the natural, if unfortunate, state of things? One would think that, even with progress in some areas, the disparities would be all the more glaring. Instead of the old social orders that had hierarchical divisions at their heart, today's democratic and liberal ones call for the equal dignity of all human beings. No longer do we respect hierarchies or any notion that some are intrinsically better than others. Today the people themselves, including women, are deemed to have the power to govern themselves. Contemporary notions of human rights insist that all people, by virtue of their membership in humanity, have equal civil and political rights. And so, women's inequality should stand out all the more as unwarranted and unjust. But sadly, instead it seems to be the norm.

And why have women allowed men to get away with this? After all, women are more than half the human population. Here the problem is twofold: one, they may have always been subordinated to men (we still don't know whether there was ever a historical moment that led to women's subordination) and, two, women do not see themselves as a group. As Simone de Beauvoir wrote, "They live dispersed among the males, attached through residence, housework, economic conditions and social standing to certain men—fathers or husbands—more firmly than they are to other women." They feel solidarity with the men of their own social, ethnic, or economic group for "the bond that unites her to her oppressors is not comparable to any other... The couple is a fundamental unity with its two halves riveted together." And so it is impossible to cleave society along the lines of sex. "Here is to be found the basic trait of woman: she is the Other in a totality of which the two components are necessary to one another."

Nonetheless, women have not entirely let men get away with this. Over the past few hundred years they created feminist movements which are both intellectual and political. As an intellectual movement, feminism is a project of investigating dominant cultural practices and their accompanying imaginaries, the ideas, metaphysical notions, and ways of seeing that lead to particular social arrangements. As a political movement, feminism has long targeted particular social arrangements that limit and harm women: fighting for equal pay and equitable treatment, for freedom from sexual harassment and violence, for civil and political rights. These movements work together, for if the ideas aren't thoroughly investigated, the arrangements that they undergird can come to seem as perfectly natural and right. For example, in order for a political movement for women's right to vote to get any traction, the intellectual work needs to be done to show that women are as capable of self-governance as men.

As an intellectual commitment and a political movement that seeks justice for women and the end of sexism in all forms, feminism is motivated by a quest for social justice. It takes up a wide range of perspectives on social, cultural, economic, and political phenomena. Nearly 250 years since Mary Wollstonecraft called for a vindication of the rights of women, feminism as both an intellectual and political movement has grown, splintered, and created new constellations of ideas and practices. As this book will show, feminist thought encompasses a huge array of areas of inquiry, philosophical and methodological points of view, and goals. Feminists agree on many basic matters, but they also disagree amongst themselves about the nature of the problem and what should be done. They differ on how to understand justice and equality, on what aspects of women's current situation are harmful or unjust. They may agree that women are unjustly being denied proper rights and respect and yet substantively differ in their accounts of how or why the injustice occurs and what is required to end it.

There is no single type of feminism. Over the past two hundred years there have been many varieties: some lauding women's distinct virtues, others proclaiming that women are just as good and capable as men. Some see the roots of women's oppression in concrete economic practices, others in deep symbolic imaginaries. On matters like pornography and prostitution, some are in favor and others adamantly against. Feminist political approaches range from liberal to libertarian, socialist to capitalist, democratic to radical.

This quick immersion into feminism will give the reader a sense of these various movements. But rather than give you a blow-by-blow account of all the theoretical debates, I decided to give you my account of feminism's story.

Chapter one begins by trying to understand the historical roots of our current situation, going back through the records of archeology and ancient myths. Was there a matriarchal era preceding patriarchy? How did patriarchy arise? And why did women's subordination to men continue in ancient and modern democratic orders, in what we might call a new fraternal order?

Chapter two traces the origins of feminist consciousness. Even though democracies continued old practices of dominating women, they inadvertently provided women with a language for freedom from domination. Along with other marginalized groups, in the eighteenth century women began to resist the fraternal order and develop a consciousness that we can now recognize as feminist.

Chapters three and four look at how sexism operates, chapter three by delineating various forms of oppression and chapter four by identifying the ideas that have passed down through the centuries that serve to keep women in their supposed place. As formidable as the various forms of oppression are—including exploitation, marginalization, and violence—the reigning ideas, what I call the metaphysics of sex, have served to make women's subordination seem natural, as just the way things are. Our contemporary cultures are still guided by archaic imaginaries, metaphysical assumptions, and their ancient grammars. By these I mean fundamental ideas about how everything hangs together, about what is better and what is worse. Over time, these ideas have become so entrenched we barely notice them.

Chapter five turns to what women want, in short, their desire, and how it can be discerned given that women's desires have for millennia been stunted and shaped by a world that diminishes them. Given all this, how can women develop the agency to identify what they really want? Given how much culture shapes identity, where is the space for women's agency? On this question I turn to resources in psychoanalysis and the possibility that we all have a "constitutional factor," that is, something in our particular temperaments, that allows us to speak back to power.

Because feminism is ultimately a social and political project, chapter six ends the book with the ethical and political question, how should we live? These include ethical questions at play in our everyday relationships and political questions about what kinds of laws and norms are best. While feminists agree on the fundamentals regarding women's control over their own bodies, many questions come up depending on the underlying feminist political philosophy, whether liberal, radical, socialist, democratic, or decolonial.

This quick immersion into feminism is meant as a dive into a huge subject. I am painfully aware of how much is not included here, especially much of the rich work carried out in the arena of analytic feminism. I have nodded to this where vital, but not turned to it fully. This is largely because of my own proclivities. I am less interested in nailing down definitions of concepts, which is a specialty of analytic philosophy, the strain of philosophy which has reigned the past fifty years in the Anglo-American world. I am more taken by the kinds of questions that continental philosophers broach, questions that are less worried about concepts and more attuned to lived experience. I know some of my analytic feminist colleagues may dispute how I characterize this, but it does seem to me that continental feminists turn more directly to what it feels like to be in a world that diminishes women than to a focus on conceptual clarity. Because of my orientation, you will see that in the later chapters I turn more squarely to these continental approaches, exemplified by the works of Luce Irigaray along with more recent scholarship by Judith Butler and Drucilla Cornell.

The further readings section offers a great deal more to read. One of the main resources I draw on is the feminist section of the *Stanford Encyclopedia of Philosophy*, which I help edit. My entry there on feminist philosophy offers a doorway into that vast resource.

Writing this book was itself a feminist adventure. I am grateful for the research assistance of Rebekah Spera whose philosophical acumen, keen eye, and way with words helped improve every chapter. I am grateful to feminist colleagues for help with key ideas as I was in the midst of working them out: Elaine Miller, Dorothea Olkowski, Mary Rawlinson, Beverly Stoute, and Cynthia Willett. I am also grateful to Katie B. Howard, my co-author for the *Stanford Encyclopedia of Philosophy* entry on feminist political philosophy, and Nancy Tuana, who drafted an earlier version of my entry on feminist philosophy. Both their ideas made their way into this book. I also am grateful to my dear friends Beth Myler, Dea Larsen, and Linda Grant for strength making it through the Covid-19 pandemic, and to my first feminist friend, Tracy Morris, for taking me to that women's conference in Houston. And finally I am grateful to my fellow board members on the feminist philosophy section of the *Stanford Encyclopedia of Philosophy*: Ann Garry, Heidi Grasswick, Serene Khader, and Anita Superson. Together we have the great honor of documenting the work of feminist philosophers worldwide.

To all my readers, I am grateful for you. Consider this book an invitation: know what came before, be attuned to what is wrong, and act on your desire to make things better. Do this for all people, past, present, and future; but first do this for yourself. The key to unlocking desire and possibilities for all is to unlock your own.

Chapter 1

Patriarchy &
The Fraternal Order

A quick immersion into feminism should begin with a chapter on what feminism is an answer to. What are the problems that feminism addresses? The feminist literature lists many, including the historical, global, and persistent problems of women's subordination, their lack of freedom, their oppression in a world in which women are treated as second-class citizens, if citizens at all. The short word that many feminists employ for this condition is "sexism" and the short term they have often enlisted to describe the condition that perpetuates it is "patriarchy."

I must admit that I am not at all satisfied with these words, *sexism* and *patriarchy*. They seem so dogmatic and simple minded. And they tend to reduce a multiplicity of things down to single phenomena and sometimes miss the larger point. Sexism is defined most simply as discrimination or prejudice on the basis of sex. That general definition leaves out multitudes, namely why it nearly universally applies to women. Gerda Lerner is more specific, defining sexism as "the ideology of male supremacy, of male superiority and of beliefs that support it." But this definition begs the question: what is an ideology? Is it something consciously shared and avowed? Must it be reigning in the current moment? My guess is that, if asked, the majority of women and men too would say and believe that the sexes are equal, different maybe, but equal. Certainly there was a time when the notion of male supremacy was widely shared, but to my mind, at least in most of the world, that time has passed.

Still, sexism is a familiar, felt phenomenon, whether in the case of a man lecturing a woman about something she already knows ("mansplaining") or finding herself stuck with cleanup duty. To the extent that these unconscious views and practices remain, women continue to be confronted with sexism. But I would not call it an ideology. The term *sexism* implies a particular intentional attitude and belief system, and often what makes life difficult for women is not someone's particular sexist beliefs but a set of prevailing structures and presuppositions. Rather than just calling something out for being sexist, I think it will be more profitable to look at people's unconscious views, the habits that remain, practices and imaginaries that are upheld by a certain order.

Should we call that order patriarchy? In this chapter I am going to offer a different term: the fraternal order. Where etymologically patriarchy means the rule (*archy*) by the father (*pater*), a fraternal order refers to an egalitarianism among men by which the norms for women's place in society are agreed to and maintained. A fraternity is closer to what Freud referred to as a band of brothers who overthrew the patriarch who had sporadically reigned in human history. But for the times in history that really concern us now, the problem is not patriarchy but the ways in which the ideals of equality and fraternity have reigned and yet still countenance women's subordination. Many feminists have pointed out the hypocrisy of these Enlightenment ideals being proclaimed to be universal while systematically denied to women (and the world's other "others"). But perhaps they are missing something obvious: at those historic times when the ideal of equality triumphed, it was not meant for women; historically it has been exclusively proclaimed by men for men: fraternity. That is a curious feature of democracy that I will come to at the end of this chapter.

But first, when and how did the communities of the world become so male dominated? When and how did women's subjugation begin? Has it always been this way or does this only occur under certain circumstances? Turning to the historical record is of little help, for history has only been recorded for a few thousand years. In all those accounts, men's rule over women was already firmly in place. If there ever was a time before male domination, it was prehistoric, and this has taken many scholars back to archaeological and other evidence. These records do not speak for themselves; they have to be interpreted.

Let's consider two broad sets of interpretations: one that there was a prehistoric time before patriarchy (or what I am calling the fraternal order) where women had as much or more power as men and another that sees scarce evidence for any such time. For the sake of brevity, I'll call the first account matriarchal and the second fraternal.

Matriarchal Accounts

The matriarchal account was first put forward by the Swiss anthropologist Johann Jakob Bachofen in his 1861 book *Mother Right: An Investigation of the Religious and Juridical Character of Matriarchy in the Ancient World*. Considered today a classic of modern anthropology, it drew on myth to posit stages of cultural development through which matriarchy was essential. In an essay titled "Bachofen's Mother Right," Justin Stagl summarizes these stages:

1) hetaerism, characterized by indiscriminate mating between all members of the primeval hordes;
2) gynecocracy (rule by women);
3) and father right

The first stage, which Bachofen posits mostly hypothetically, was precultural. There was no law or ethics. Maternal-child bonds provided some stability against an otherwise anarchic social world. But women were still subject to male aggression. "The transition from hetaerism to gynecocracy," Stagl explains, "means the ascent from a 'precultural' to a 'cultural stage' and a first step towards spiritualization," that is, the ultimate stage of patriarchy or father right. The second stage, gynecocracy, which Bachofen also calls matriarchy proper, "owes its appearance to women: 'Defenceless against abuse by men, and … exhausted by their lusts, women was first to feel the need for regulated conditions and a purer ethic.'"

Later, fraternal accounts, which I will turn to later in this chapter, also posit a possible pre-cultural state where men exercised brute power. As we'll see, these fraternal accounts claim that something like a band of brothers wrested power away from such alpha males and in favor of cultural norms, that is, toward what we recognize now as properly human. Bachofen's account was radical in seeing the transition from more animal to more human culture as the work of women.

While he saw great value in early matriarchal cultures, for Bachofen the most evolved stage was the third one in which patriarchy was finally achieved. Matriarchy was still tethered to matter and world, but patriarchy was a move to transcendence and spirituality. Despite Bachofen's ultimate preference for patriarchy, in giving motherhood such a central role in development, Bachofen gave many women's advocates a new cause: maternalism. In the nineteenth century feminists in England and North America championed how maternal instincts made women more altruistic and virtuous. A hundred years later, feminist scholars started using archeological records to pinpoint a time of matriarchy.

For several decades now, many feminist theorists have been continuing this line of inquiry into how male domination of women came to be. To name a few, Gerda Lerner's book, *The Creation of Patriarchy*, came out in 1986; Riane Eisler's *The Chalice & the Blade* in 1987; and Marilyn French's *From Eve to Dawn: A History of Women* in 2002. Of them, only Lerner even mentions Bachofen, but they all follow his notion that early hunter-gatherer societies were more egalitarian or even matriarchal rather than patriarchal. They acknowledge that there were indeed gendered divisions of labor but, they argue, these were seen as equally valuable and necessary. Many of the matriarchal texts argue that woman's procreative power was revered and even worshipped, giving rise to female deities. They argue that family lineages were matrilineal, that violence was rare, and hierarchy all but absent.

Many of the matriarchal histories point to the more egalitarian roles that men and women had during paleolithic eras, at least what we can discern from the archaeological data. Like other mammals, female humans gave birth and were their children's primary caregivers. But this did not automatically associate with lower status. Many, but not all, hunter-gatherer societies had divisions of labor, with women doing more gathering and men more hunting, but, the historians of matriarchy hold, both men and women were seen as equally valuable members of the community. Lerner notes that all the available data indicate that members of hunter-gatherer societies were interdependent. "A woman must secure the services of a hunter in order to be assured of a meat supply for herself and her children. A hunter must be assured of a woman who will supply him with subsistence for the hunt and in the event the hunt is unsuccessful." So long as there is mutually interdependence, a gendered division of labor need not be sexist. The trouble comes when one group is rendered dependent on the other.

The matriarchal accounts also posit that because the biology of reproduction was still largely a mystery, women's reproductive power was held in awe. Largely a mystery, it signaled women's divine power to create life, becoming a model for divinity itself. "It is from the Neolithic that we derive surviving evidence of cave paintings and sculptures suggesting the pervasive veneration of the Mother-Goddess," Lerner writes. This makes sense given the psychological bond between infant and mother, where in the early days the child is utterly dependent on her for its survival. Given this "dramatic and mysterious power of the female," men and women "turned to the veneration of the Mother-Goddess."

The matriarchal view identifies several factors that led to the end of this idyllic arrangement.

First was male jealousy of women's procreative power, resulting in men appropriating to themselves patrimony over children and eventually the concept of men being the ultimate creators. In addition to the material ways in which men came to dominate women, Gerda Lerner documents the ways in which men appropriated women's reproductive power. For Aristotle, women were mere matter but men's seed provided the form of life. Men were the active producers and creators, women passive, not creators at all. These spurious biologies gave rise to symbolic systems, ways of seeing the world more broadly: "On the basis of such symbolic constructs, embedded in Greek philosophy, the Judeo-Christian theologies, and the legal tradition on which Western civilization is built," Lerner writes, "men have explained the world in their own terms and defied the important questions so as to make themselves the center of discourse."

A second step was the creation of male solidarity. Marilyn French's account turns to hunting practices in a way that dovetails with the band-of-brothers' story. But instead of being a way to overturn a despotic leader, she sees hunting practices as a way for men to exert control over women. French follows the view that early hunter/gatherer societies and early simple agricultural communities were already egalitarian and centered around mothers. "The shift from female centrality to male domination occurred before the development of writing, so its roots are hidden," French writes. But likely, she says, it emerged from male hostility to women and was nourished through the creation of male solidarity. "Perhaps hunting, on which male anthropologists place so much weight, gave men a sense of identity, responsibility, and power." Through hunting, men had to focus on cooperation, not competition, but they could together exclude women from the bond. "If men had felt marginal, cooperation during hunts may have provided an exclusive sense of maleness and solidarity."

That worked fine so long as there was enough big game to hunt, but by 5000 BCE, French notes, in populated areas game was beginning to vanish and men found themselves farming more. To make up for the loss of solidarity through hunting, men in these horticultural societies devised new rituals, puberty rites, group initiations which taught male gender roles. As French writes,

> Male solidarity was and remains a mobilization against women. The first political movement, it arose, like all solidarity movements, to counter a sense of powerlessness and oppression. (The notion that men suffer from envy of female

procreativity has long been a theme in psychology.) The main thrust of group initiations is denying the mother and all the qualities associated with her: nutritiveness, compassion, softness, and love. Boys are taught to scorn "feminine" emotions, replacing them with hardness, self-denial, obedience, and deference to "superior" males, creating a bond not of love but of power directed at transcendent goals.

The most brutal initiations occurred in the most male-dominant societies. "To wean a boy from his beloved mother and teach him to dominate women, men brutalize him: they take boys from society for weeks or longer, subjecting them to prolonged humiliation and mutilation." We can see vestiges of these initiation rites in the hazing rituals in college fraternities, male solidarity, modern-day bands of brothers.

A third factor is the rise of agriculture, entailing a move from a nomadic existence in which men and women are interdependent to a more stratified society. Where the division of labor among hunter-gatherer societies was largely egalitarian, patriarchy emerged with the rise of agriculture in this Neolithic period. Depending on the kinds of crops being grown and the tools needed to tend to them, men's labor might become more valuable. As people began to grow more than they needed to live, they began to store and trade. Money arose. Wealth increased. Those with more wealth became more powerful. Societies became more complex and political power more formalized.

With complex societies comes the fourth factor: war. Even in Plato's *Republic*, as Socrates and his fellows muse over how a comfortable society might be constructed, they quickly gravitate to the need for soldiers to protect the state and grab more land when their own is insufficient. As the feminist historians see it, the new "warrior" ideal created the possibility that some people might dominate others, that strength could justify domination. And why look abroad when one could find at home a handy division of strong and weak.

With war comes the taking of prisoners. Wars led to prisoners of war, largely women. Households reflected the warrior mentality of male domination. And what the anthropologist Claude Lévi-Strauss called "the exchange of women" as well as the commodification of their sexual and reproductive capacities gave rise to men's exploitation of women, including their sexual services. With the beginning of agriculture, women became spoils of war, enslaved for their reproduction and labor. Also they became ways that men could pay off their debts, hiring out their wives or daughters. "The product of this commodification of women—bride price, sale price and children—was appropriated by men," Lerner writes, perhaps the first step toward the accumulation of private property, as well as the first step toward class differences.

As Lerner puts it, male prisoners of war would often be killed, but women prisoners of war would be kept alive, made into slaves, perhaps the very first instance of private property. Some have argued that patriarchy arose with the development of private property. But the historical record shows that patriarchy came first, giving rise to the first from of private property: men owning women, not just as slaves but also as wives and prostitutes. A society that enforces women as property renders women dependent on men.

Luce Irigaray draws on Marx and Engels to point out the consequences of the founding of private property in the household:

> For the patriarchal order is indeed the one that functions as the *organization and monopolization of private property for the benefit of the head of the family*. It is his proper name, the name of the father, that determines ownership for the family, including the wife and children. And what is required of them—for the wife, monogamy; for the children, the precedence of the male line, and specifically of the eldest son who bears the name—is also required so as to ensure "the concentration of considerable wealth in the hands of a single individual—a man" and to "bequeath this wealth to the children of that man and of no other."

A fifth factor is religion, especially the development of monotheism. Instead of the creative capacity of women and mother-goddesses to create life, monotheism vests this power in a single divine and purportedly male figure who has a concept. This dovetails with the first factor, men's jealousy of women's productive power. The roots of this go back to Old Mesopotamian myths, including one in which "the creating god mentally defines the nature-to-be of his creation: when it has taken final shape in his imagination and he has given it a name, he draws its shape, whereby it acquired almost complete life." Well before the book of Genesis was written, Lerner notes, "the concept of creation has changed, at a certain period in history, from being merely the acting out of the mystic force of female fertility to being a conscious act of creation." These new concepts arise at the same time that writing is being invented. "The symbolification of the capacity to create…simplifies the move away from the Mother-Goddess as the sole principle of creativity."

Eventually the divine power of creation would move from the fecundity of the earth and bodies to the divine and rational capacity to create new ideas and concepts. And, in the process, it would be stripped from women altogether and vested in Man. As Rosemary Radford Ruether explains, "The foundational thinker of Latin Christianity, St. Augustine, in the late fourth and early fifth centuries established certain assumptions that still plague

Catholicism. Although Augustine acknowledged that women possessed the image of God and were redeemable, he believed that as *feminae* or females they were created by God from the beginning to be under male subjugation. Women's disproportionate guilt for the fall of humanity into sin, rooted in women's disobedience to their subordination, meant that women could only be redeemed by accepting a redoubled subjugation to the male, even coercively so. For Augustine the female could never represent God. Maleness was the appropriate image of rationality and spirituality, while the feminine represented the body and the material world."

So now a single force, God's will, is the source of creativity. In the Hebrew Bible, God contracts with Adam alone, excluding Eve, and continues to mediate through men only. Only men can become priests and only men can take part in the most sacred rituals. As Genevieve Lloyd explains in her essay, "The Man of Reason,"

> Much of the debate in this Renaissance "war of the sexes" was conducted in theological terms, centering on the exegesis of Genesis. And what prevailed, in terms of the Genesis debate, was that Man was made in God's image. And that woman was made as his literal and metaphorical "offsider". Whether she also was made fully in the likeness of God paled into social insignificance

compared with the fact that her role was to be man's companion and helpmate and hence subject to his rule.

As the Judeo-Christian theologies develop, they fold in ancient Greek philosophical ideas—first from Plato and then from Aristotle—that further exclude women from sacred and symbolic practices. From Plato they took the twin ideas that bodily sense perception is inferior to rational thought and that the body dragged down the soul. In the first century AD, the Jewish scholar and theologian, Philo of Alexandria, connected Platonic thought to the story of Genesis. "Echoing Plato," Lloyd writes, Philo "presented sense perception as the source of disorders of the soul, giving rise to a tide of passions which threatens to engulf sovereign reason." Philo drew on both the Genesis account of the relation of Adam and Eve and Plato's notion that reason could be corrupted if it relied upon the senses. He concluded that, as Lloyd writes, "Woman, symbolizing sense perception, becomes the source of the fall for man, symbolizing mind."

In the fourth century AD, Augustine also drew on Plato. However, unlike Plato, Augustine interprets women's seemingly natural physical subordination to men as corresponding to the superiority of the intellect to the senses. As Lloyd puts it, women's subordination "represents rational control, the subjection of flesh to spirit in the moral life." Notice that Augustine is taking the subordination of women as natural and then folds that into Christian theology. As Gerda Lerner explains, "By the time men began symbolically to order the universe and the relationship of humans to God in major explanatory systems, the subordination of women had become so completely accepted that it appeared 'natural' both to men and women."

Later Christian thought drew on Aristotle to the same effect, but now instead of a metaphysics of mind over matter, Christianity draws on a metaphysics of function. Where a man's "vital functioning" is to be in the image of God, Lloyd explains, a woman's function is to serve man. Again, the philosophers take for granted something that came earlier, women's domination, and then they further entrench women's subordination by making it a central element in the symbolic systems of the past two millennia.

While I would not call Genevieve Lloyd or Gerda Lerner maternalists, their accounts of the development of symbolic systems of religion are in keeping with a maternalist account of how patriarchy came to supplant any early matriarchal social organizations. Along with male jealousy of women's power, male solidarity in the hunt, and then the rise of agriculture, war, and property, religious systems solidified women's subordination. In the matriarchal accounts, no one of these factors alone spelled doom for matriarchy, but together they effectively supplanted it with a new patriarchal order.

The matriarchal view has received a mixed reception. While many feminist theologians and maternalists, wanting to celebrate women's traditional roles, seem to like it very much, other feminists find parts of the account troubling. For one, some are put off by what seems to be the maternalist view that there are in fact innate, perhaps biological, differences between the sexes that make women more nurturing. Perhaps these attributes are products of a sexist culture and should not be celebrated as the feature of one sex rather than another. For another, some find that the scholarship behind the matriarchal view is wanting. In her 2000 book, *The Myth of Matriarchal Prehistory*, Cynthia Eller debunks key pillars of the theory: one being the notion that human beings were ignorant of men's role in procreation until relatively recently and the other being the fast and loose way that much archaeological evidence has been interpreted. It is indeed possible, Eller grants, that there might have been matriarchal cultures, but it is hardly a fact.

Fraternal Accounts

Bachofen's matriarchal account of 1861 may be a classic of anthropology theory but its evidence leaves much to be desired. Today's anthropologists may consult myths, but they also look to the archaeological record, to contemporary hunter-gatherer societies that have been relatively untouched

by modern society, and to our primate cousins—
chimpanzees, bonobos, gorillas, and orangutans—to
get some clues about what very early human society
might have been like. Of the primates, bonobos are
generally an egalitarian bunch, but we *homo sapiens*
are closer genetically to chimpanzees, which does not
bode well. Chimp communities are often led by an
alpha male, a leader who controls all access to food
and females and can be quite violent. In chimpanzee
communities, mothers feed their children but the
rest of the community keeps food for themselves. The
males in the community are stratified from the one
alpha to middle and lower hierarchies. Dominant
males maintain their position through displays of
aggression and violence.

But it turns out that our primate cousins are a very
poor indicator of early human societies. As Bruce M.
Knauft has shown, in simple hunter-gatherer societies
of the late Paleolithic era, "the pervasive ethos is one
of active cooperative affiliation among diverse groups
of relatives and nonrelatives." As Knauft explains,

> Perhaps the most striking thing about simple
> human societies is how decentralized they
> are. Instead of individuals' striving to be
> "first among equals," aggressively assertive, or
> powerful-striving to be big-men, there tends
> to be active and assiduous devaluation of adult
> male status differentiation and minimization
> or denial of those asymmetries of ability

that exist. Self-aggrandizing behavior is disparaged and open coercion considered highly improper... Leadership is rudimentary and uninstitutionalized, and political life is communal. Patriarchy and elders' authority are minimal, and leadership is itself rarely a matter of assertion, dispute, or competition. Decisions are most frequently reached through casual consensus, in which no man has authority over another. Major collective enterprises tend to emerge spontaneously as the result of myriad fluid conversations that mix stories, banter, fantasies, and plans. As Ingold... points out, politics in simple societies maintains a fine balance between individual autonomy and the collective appropriation of nature.

But over time, as those societies become more complex, sedentary, and wealthy, the communities become more stratified and inegalitarian. The men in the group start vying for power, wealth, and status. Some communities begin to condone men, namely the rich and powerful ones, having more than one wife. In short, the men in those communities start behaving more like our chimpanzee cousins.

Knauft calls this the U-shaped curve. Through our primate and early human history, at the start with our chimpanzee cousins, male status differentiation was very high; in late paleolithic communities, there was very little if any status differentiation between men; but in the Neolithic era as communities became more sedentary, complex, and wealthy, the status differentials between men increased enormously. The simple hunter-gatherer societies of the late paleolithic era seems to be most peaceful and egalitarian, with very firm norms of sharing. But this is a society of equals only of men. In all the societies men reigned over women. At both ends of the U-shaped curve, a small elite group, perhaps just one alpha-male, has access to all the women. At the bottom of the curve, along with sharing food and power, all the men share the women.

Towards Equality... Between Men

We must pause here and note that Knauft's account of the rise and fall of egalitarian societies was not an account of equality between the sexes. It was an account of the power differences between men. At one extreme there was a very patriarchal culture, in which an elite alpha man/men had power versus, at another end, men shared power more equally.

Even as limited, and disappointing, as this account of equality is, an interesting question is how did early human societies topple the alpha male? The span of time from chimp to human is vast, and it is hard to know exactly what happened. But one view is that to become human homo sapiens had to learn to communicate, cooperate, and coordinate. Hunting big game required this. And the riches that might have been had by winning alone paled in the face of the risks of going it alone. Human survival would necessitate sharing and cooperation; it would require toppling any alpha males.

Robert A. Paul, an anthropologist and psychoanalyst, notes the similarities in Knauft's account and Sigmund Freud's account in his quasi-anthropological text, *Totem and Taboo*. There Freud notes a similar transition in human history from rule by the father (who kept all the women to himself) to rule by a band of brothers who kill the father and then create norms and practices whereby the women would be shared among them. In *Totem and Taboo*, Freud states that this happened at one point in human pre-history and that ever since then men have remembered that event and, out of guilt, created taboos, such as the incest taboo, to order their affairs. But later he writes that this event likely happened over and over again such that its memory carried down through generations. In a 2010 journal article, "Yes, the Primal Crime Did Take Place," Paul argues that Freud's seemingly outlandish story does in fact fit well with anthropological research, namely Knauft's "U-shaped curve": First, there were very early humans, who like their chimpanzee relatives probably lived in groups led by a "primal father" or "alpha male" who controlled all the resources. Second, those groups killed off the role of the alpha male and its hierarchical organization in order to have more egalitarian societies where people lived together more cooperatively. But third, as these communities developed and began entering into wars with others and resources became more fought over, hierarchy developed again.

That second "moment" likely lasted for hundreds of thousands of years. Paul follows Christopher Boehm's view that the egalitarianism of that period did not come about gradually but likely "was a literal and dramatic reversal of the dominance hierarchy" of the previous era. "Instead of there being a single alpha who dominates a group of subordinates who show deference" while they bide their time in hopes of climbing up the hierarchy, "there is in a human band society a community of horizontally equivalent members who collectively, under the banner of a moral ideology opposed to self-assertion, are able to dominate any would-be alpha who puts himself forward."

Again, note that in both the anthropological accounts and the Freudian one, this "human band society" that overthrows the alpha male is really a society of men. Paul observes that the capacity for deposing alpha males may have developed in large hunting parties, which were mostly comprised of men. There they developed skills of communication and cooperation, along with solidarity. They also developed a new idea of living together in an egalitarian manner. Paul quotes Freud, "the first demand made by this reaction-formation [against jealousy of sibling rivals] is the demand for justice, for equal treatment for all... If one cannot be the favourite oneself, at all events nobody else shall be the favourite." They would find ways to be equal in how they shared their women.

Does this fraternal account preclude a matriarchal account? Having read Bachofen, Freud thinks not. In a 1919 letter to Lou Andreas-Salomé, Freud writes, "I have long had unexpressed ideas on the question of matriarchy. Where is one to place it? I think, on the basis of the totem-taboo hypothesis, in the period after the fall of the primal father, the period in which the male had not yet brought himself to the point of founding a secondary family, in which therefore the dominant role now fell as a matter of course upon the shoulders of the woman, who had lost her master. Unfortunately, I find it impossible to ascribe a date to the whole early history of the family, although I know that this is essential, if one is to give it its full significance in relation to the other phases of the development of the family."

In their books, the matriarchal theorists do not begin with a band-of-brothers story and they generally use the language of patriarchy, not fraternity. But their story does pick up where Freud leaves it, at the point before founding the secondary family. If there was a matriarchal moment in history, it is swallowed up by a larger one, where the men find equality in their ways of divvying up the women.

But here I think the story of what happened at the start and through most of those tens of thousands of years of prehistory gets complicated. How much of the move to egalitarianism was the work of a band of brothers? And how much was it the work of interdependent communities of men and women and children? Even more daunting, how much are both the matriarchal and the band of brothers stories retroactive fantasies and self-fulfilling prophecies? Both stories feature men as the primary big-game hunters. As it turns out, recently archeologists discovered the 9,000-year-old burial sites of a female big game hunter in the Andes. As a result, some went back to other burial sites of hunters presumed to be men and now, with better scientific methods, they discovered that 26 of 107 hunters were actually women. As Annalee Newitz wrote in the January 1, 2021 *New York Times*,

> Bonnie Pitblado, an archaeologist at the University of Oklahoma, Norman, told Science magazine that the findings indicate that "women have always been able to hunt and have in fact hunted." The new data calls into question an influential dogma in the field of archaeology. Nicknamed "man the hunter," this is the notion that

men and women in ancient societies had strictly defined roles: Men hunted, and women gathered. Now, this theory may be crumbling.

Screen Memories

Ironically, the matriarchal theory is just as guilty as any other account of presuming that, for the most part, men were the hunters. The archaeological and fossil records do not speak for themselves. They must be interpreted— and it is all too easy to import one's general views of things into an interpretation. This is the problem with any attempt to construct a genesis story of events when there is no living memory of it. We can use fragments of memories and data to tell ourselves stories about how things began; but into these stories we can introduce recent experience. Freud calls these "screen memories" where, unconsciously, recent memories get imprinted on to old ones. In the case of the "man the hunter" story, it may well be that our current experience of the fraternal order gets smuggled into assumptions about what the pre-historic, that is, namely paleolithic, division of labor must have been. We are on firmer ground as we move into trying to interpret the Neolithic story, though by then patriarchy was well in place.

Democracy and the Fraternal Order

Knauft's account ends in the early millennia of the Neolithic era, perhaps about 12,000 to 10,000 years ago. We know from historical accounts that inequality kept increasing, empires formed, tyrants led. At the same time, there were cultures that seemed to afford more cooperation and joy between the sexes, such as Minoan Crete, but even it too was overrun by invaders as well as natural disasters. By the beginning of the sixth century BCE, even the most advanced societies were ruled by powerful men. But then something extraordinary happened: democracy. In 598 BCE the Athenian politician Cleisthenes transformed political power from the clan, headed by a patriarch, to the deme, where all property-owning men were one among equals. While in ancient Greece and Rome the male head of the household had full legal authority over the household's women and children, for a few hundred years in Athens after 598 BCE things were different. The city itself ceased to be governed by a patriarchal logic. What ruled society was not the father's—or the clan leader's—brute power but the rule of law, law constituted by men who saw themselves as equals.

After Cleisthenes' political reforms, the right of a man to rule his household is not based on patriarchal power but on a politically given right, a larger social order—that of men—granting men dominion over women and children. Mary

Rawlinson suggests that, instead of *patriarchy*, we call this form of rule *fraternity*. As she writes in her book, *Just Life*, "Philosophy in the West, including political philosophy, is built upon the foundation of a mythological violence: … the brothers kill the father in order to redistribute his wealth, his property, and his women. Fraternity is installed as the controlling political structure to contain the violence and protect the privileges of property. Henceforth, patriarchy is set within it." Or as Juliet Flower MacCannell puts it, "What we have in the place of the patriarchy is the Regime of the Brother."

I agree, and I would add that in Athens of the sixth century emerges a radically new social form—democracy—that supplants patriarchal rule for the political society, but it doesn't supplant rule by men over women in the household. Instead, it changes what authorizes men's rule over women. "The father's authority over the family depends on the recognition of it by other male heads-of-household," Rawlinson writes, "The lateral relations of fraternity sustain the vertical or hierarchical relations of patriarchy." As Rawlinson puts it, from a feminist point of view, this is no longer male rule over women based on the logic of the clan or the horde, it is the logic of collective agreement of those who get *counted* as equal. In other words, the primary problem is not patriarchy but a political order that supports it: the fraternal order. As democracy "flourished" in Athens, women lacked any standing in the household or in the polis.

Chapter 2
Feminist Consciousness

Democracy's Irony

The democratic fraternal order of ancient Athens lasted a few hundred years and then was overturned by the patriarchal logic of empire: from that of the empire of Alexander the Great through the Holy Roman Empire, then Byzantium, and finally the Ottoman Empire. In Greece and elsewhere, for over a thousand years, there was little democratic imagination. But in the seventeenth and eighteenth centuries AD, a new band of brothers emerged calling for what came to be the hallmark ideals of the Enlightenment: *liberté, egalité, fraternité*. Their genesis included John Locke calling for liberal governance based on consent of those involved, Jean Jacques Rousseau saying that only the General Will of the people should rule, and Immanuel Kant calling for people to wake up and shake off tutelage. In quick succession, at the end of the eighteenth century, came the American and then the French Revolutions. During the nineteenth century more nations throughout Europe formed liberal, democratic governments, and colonized nations in Latin America began gaining independence. In the twentieth century, colonized peoples on the African continent began to get their own independence.

None of this was perfect, but for the most part the era of patriarchal power by unelected leaders came to an end. But rather than these principles serving to liberate all of humanity, oddly they kept in place patriarchal power in the private sphere. Through the beginning years of this democratic awakening, the Enlightenment principles of freedom and equality became the foundations for Europe colonizing the New World and profiting from the slave trade. They served to justify colonization, domination, and the continued subjugation of women. How so? By narrowly defining what it was to be human and civilized and thus justifying ruling over others to help "bring them up" to civilized ideals.

Were it not for the women's movements that began forming in the nineteenth century in countries around the globe, women would continue to be second class citizens, if citizens at all. As Carole Pateman argues in her book, *The Sexual Contract*, the very same Lockean theory of consent that led to men's liberation from aristocracy served to create a brotherhood among men who could rule over women. It transferred the right of domination from the patriarchal king/ fathers to the democratic brothers. And as Charles Mills notes in his book, *The Racial Contract*, these very same principles undergirded the institutions of colonialism and slavery.

In the new United States of America, freedom and equality were only guaranteed to landed white men. Instead of being beholden to a king, now they were accountable to each other. All these men were equal to each other in their freedom to mind their own private affairs, which included whatever happened in their own households. Again, democracy did not improve the condition for all the people. Instead it created a new fraternal order and authority for male rule over women, which reined largely without interruption well into the late twentieth century when, throughout the world, male heads of household still had control over the household. Women could not get a bank account or a credit card in their own name, they could not file for divorce, and "marital rape" was taken to be an oxymoron — for, until the 1990s, a marriage license was taken as license for a husband to forcibly have sex with his wife whenever he wanted.

Resistance

But while the new democratic band of brothers may have wanted to save these Enlightenment ideals for themselves alone, they met resistance from the start. Throughout the world, despite the fraternal order's desire to keep the new liberties to themselves, once they were proclaimed and lauded, oppressed peoples started engaging in "immanent critique," that is, the practice of criticizing a society in light of its own ideals. The introduction of ideals of freedom and equality, even if meant for only some, meant that those ideals were circulating broadly. They became aspirational for others. If "all men are created equal," why aren't women and people of color equal as well? Immanent critique is not just a matter of finding fault with the status quo; it is a way to change it, to expand the club of who benefits from the society's own ideals.

The French Revolution of 1789 was born in response to the tyranny of the *ancien regime*. The revolutionaries called for the rights of man, and indeed men alone. Its founding document of August 1789, The Declaration of the Rights of Man and of the Citizen, proclaimed that men were citizens and women were not. In October 1789, with the price of bread rising and famine looming, a group of market women gathered, then expanded into the thousands as they marched on Versailles, demanding that the king and his family return to Paris to live among the people. Emboldened by their victory, these "mothers of the French Revolution," presented to the National Constituent Assembly a petition to the National Assembly calling for the abolition of male privilege, equality between the sexes, the end of male rule within the household, and a host of other measures, all echoing the language of the Declaration of the Rights of Man and of the Citizen. One of thousands of petitions to the Assembly, it was left on the table.

We could say that mothers of the French Revolution were engaging in immanent critique. They took the society's own ideals and tried to make them more fully real. So too did Marie-Olympe de Gouges, a feminist playwright and intellectual of the French revolution, following the creation of the French constitution of 1791 which also ignored women's calls for political rights, leaving out any rights for women to vote, to have any equality in marriage, to divorce, or own property, in response, Marie-Olympe de Gouges published a manifesto, "The Rights of Women." In it she offered a lengthy list of rights for women, drawing on the very language of the National Assembly's Declaration of the Rights of Man. And then in a postscript she adds, "Woman, wake up! The tocsin of reason is being heard throughout the whole universe; discover your rights." Now that the flame of truth has dispersed the clouds of folly, she writes, enslaved men still need women's strength to break his chains. "Having become free, he has become unjust to his companion." Marie-Olympe de Gouges hoped the National Assembly would take up her proposal but instead, two years later, at the start of the reign of terror, she was imprisoned and then, during the terror, executed.

The irony of all men being equal but women not led to some awakenings, ultimately leading to the subject of this book: feminism, which at its most basic level is a call for women's equality. Writing in England during the time of the French Revolution, Mary Wollstonecraft tended to agree with the fraternal order that men seemed more rational than women, but she blamed this situation on women's lack of education. In her 1792 essay, "A Vindication of the Rights of Women," she wrote, "I attribute [these problems] to a false system of education, gathered from the books written on this subject by men, who, considering females rather as women than human creatures, have been more anxious to make them alluring mistresses than affectionate wives and rational mother... [T]he civilised women of this present century, with a few exceptions, are only anxious to inspire love, when they ought to cherish a nobler ambition, and by their abilities and virtues exact respect."

Writing in an era of revolutionary fervor, Wollstonecraft joined the demand for women's equality to men's demand for political equality. This call for equality is two-fold: it is both a call for what is the case and a call for what ought to be the case, or as philosophers put it, it is both normative and descriptive. Normatively we could say that women have as much intrinsic worth as men and ought to be treated as such. Descriptively, one can document all the ways in which they are treated unequally and lack the basic rights and living conditions that the other sex has. Together, these claims show how wrong it is to treat women as less than men. If women were less capable than men to decide how to live their own lives, then there would not be anything wrong with treating them as inferior. But if they do have moral worth and with it the right to decide their own ends, then they ought to be treated as such. As these early feminists were arguing, doing anything less is immoral. Together the normative and descriptive claims provide reasons for working politically to change the way things are.

It was not just in Europe and the United States that women were beginning to make these demands for change. Women have been resisting various manifestations of the fraternal order all over the world. In the West, feminist history and theory are often taught as if feminism was solely a Western invention. But the truth is that, there have been women's movements for freedom for the past two centuries in all parts of the world, including Asia, Latin America, Africa, the Middle East, and the Pacific Islands. I list some of these here just to give a sense of how global feminism is—and how shared the concerns are.

In the nineteenth century, one main concern was that women did in fact seem to be inferior to men: women were less accomplished, less educated, less rational and dispassionate. The fraternal order offered all this as evidence of women's lesser abilities, but women's advocates argued that this was a result of women's inferior education, their lack of opportunity, and their apparent weakness, not just physically but socially. In response, one theme shared in women's struggles around the world was to show that these differences were not the result of nature endowing men with more than women, but of a culture that denied women educational and other opportunities to develop their strengths. So they called for education.

In China during the late nineteenth century, missionaries set up schools for their own girls and then Chinese reformers worked to create the first school for girls, which opened in 1897. These schools helped create a cadre of women's advocates working for freedom from imperialism and for national liberation, as well as for causes that directly affected women, including a marriage resistance movement, "antimarriage associations" of women who lived together collectively.

In England in 1861, John Stuart Mill published *The Subjection of Women*, which includes many ideas of his late wife, Harriett Taylor Mill, who had published a book calling for the enfranchisement of women. "I deny that any one knows or can know, the nature of the two sexes," Mill writes, "as long as they have only been seen in their present relation to one another. Until conditions of equality exist, no one can possibly assess the natural differences between women and men, distorted as they have been. What is natural to the two sexes can only be found out by allowing both to develop and use their faculties freely."

In India, the world's most populous democracy, Devaki Jain writes that regardless of caste, and regardless of how venerated female figures are in religious domains, "The truth is that women are powerless in Indian society; worse, the value given to them even as physical beings is particularly low." Beginning in the late nineteenth century, upper-caste women, bristling at how the British colonizers looked down on India, worked to improve the condition of women, first focusing on women's education. Over time, women of other castes joined the movement, engaged in social reform. The movement was complicated by nationalist struggles for independence, including resistance against colonial calls for "modernizing" the Hindu family.

Another aspect of women's resistance is that it often intersected with working against other forms of oppression. The women of the French Revolution decried France's role in slavery, the women of India worked to find common cause across castes, Chinese women worked for both women's empowerment and national liberation from feudalism. In the United States during the nineteenth century the struggles for women's rights and the abolition of slavery intersected.

Two of the founders of what would come to be known as the "first wave" of feminism, Lucretia Mott and Elizabeth Cady Stanton, met in 1840 in London for an international antislavery meeting that they attended with their husbands. As women, they were only allowed to observe, not participate. So on their ship home they started planning to hold a convention for women. Along with a group of Quaker women, they held in 1848 what came to be the first women's convention in the United States, the Seneca Falls Convention. At the meeting they produced "The Declaration of Sentiments." Echoing the language of the U.S. Declaration of Independence, it was another example of immanent critique, declaring that all men and women are equal and have inalienable rights. At the urging of the one African American person attending the meeting, the famous abolitionist Frederick Douglass, the declaration included a call for women's right to vote.

At its start, the U.S. women's movement was largely a movement of and by white women. A few years after the Seneca Falls meeting, the former slave and powerful orator Sojourner Truth called out the way that the newly emerging women's movement was uninterested in the situation of black women. As she put it in a speech in 1851, "That man over there says that women need to be helped into carriages, and lifted over ditches, and to have the best place everywhere. Nobody ever helps me into carriages, or over mud-puddles, or gives me any best place! And ain't I a woman?" Despite Sojourner Truth's powerful question, the U.S. women's movement in this first wave mostly focused on the rights of white women, culminating in the passage of the 19th Amendment. Fully ratified in August 1920, the 19th Amendment to the U.S. Constitution declares that "the right of citizens of the United States to vote shall not be denied or abridged by the United States or by any State on account of sex." As important as that victory was, it did not address the other ways that the right to vote could be denied or abridged: Jim Crow, the practice of denying the vote to people of color, including Black women. So the 19th Amendment was a victory for white women, but left many other people still denied this fundamental right.

Outside the United States, as the nineteenth century came to a close and the twentieth century began, feminist resistance gained traction around the world. These feminist waves and struggles were not imported "from outside" through colonial expansion, but were continuations of movements that were already developing in countries such as Turkey, Egypt, Afghanistan, India, Sri Lanka, Indonesia, the Philippines, China, Vietnam, Korea, and Japan.

In Latin America, the first concerted feminist movements and waves of activism came about in the late nineteenth and early twentieth century, with women struggling for equality and political participation as well as social transformations more broadly, particularly after the Mexican revolution. There were women's movements in Argentina, Colombia, and Chile, among others. In Colombia during World War II, women game together as a multiethnic, cross-class coalition to struggle for equal political participation and formed the *Unión Femenina de Colombia*, a political and mutual aid group for women. In 1930 Georgina Fletcher founded the IV International Women's Congress. It was attended by both men and women, becoming Colombian women's first public voice. Over the next six years, women gained entry to political offices and began to advocate for women's education (founding a women's university) and suffrage, which was finally won in 1954.

Luz Helena Sánchez, in an essay published in Robin Morgan's 1984 volume, *Sisterhood is Global*, describes the situation of feminist movements in Latin America later in the twentieth century. Latin American "New Feminism" emerged in the 1970s, she writes, and it involved "a struggle for autonomy vis à vis the structures of patriarchal power." Many of the women involved in these movements were students, political activists, and trade-unionists. Some were academics who wanted to research women's situation, new forms of creativity, and ways to counter sexual violence against women. In 1981 they achieved a long dream of creating a continent-wide organization, the Latin American and Caribbean Association for the Study of Women.

In the 1960s, the countries of continental Africa embarked on an exhilarating period of decolonialization, freeing themselves of their colonial rulers and beginning their own projects of democratic self-rule. (Alas, most of the continent's resources stayed in colonial hands, so the pillage continued and the results weren't as profound as hoped.) At the time, African men engaged in these liberation struggles tacitly acknowledged women's own calls for liberation, but said, basically, "wait, there are other issues more urgent." To this, the Nigerian feminist Molara Ogundipe-Leslie responded: "Somehow, miraculously, you can liberate a country and later turn your attention to the women of that country —first things first! But … no basic and effective change can occur in a society without the synchronic liberation of its women… Women's liberation is about the fundamental human rights of women in all areas of life, public and private."

When white women in the United States finally won the right to vote in 1920, the first wave of feminism rolled back into the sea, with much else in women's life remaining largely the same. In the 1940s many women entered into the job market to make a living and help with the war effort while their spouses were fighting World War II. During the 1950s, the backlash was strong, with cinched waists and aprons replacing the garb of Rosie the Riveter.

The second wave of feminism began in earnest in the 1960s. One of the many groups was The New York Radical Women's organization, founded by Shulamith Firestone and Pam Allen. It introduced a new technique, borrowing from the Old Left:

consciousness-raising groups. These could take place in someone's living room or kitchen, a gathering where participants took turns speaking about and reflecting on their daily experiences. They began to develop concepts that allowed them to articulate their experiences of sexism. Take what was a common experience of a woman walking down the street and getting catcalls and whistles, "hey babies," and other general noises and comments about her body. These were supposed to be compliments, affirmations that a woman was indeed desirable. In a consciousness-raising group, someone might try to explain what it actually really felt like. It didn't feel like being complimented, she might say. It felt like being treated like a thing, an object. And in this way women started putting their experiences into a new frame, to develop a feminist consciousness. This was not a compliment, it was being "objectified," treated like a thing. By putting experience into words and creating new concepts to describe their experience, participants could become more conscious of what was happening to them and how wrong it was.

Another part of feminist work was literary. At the start of feminism's second wave, Betty Friedan wrote what would become a huge bestseller, *The Feminine Mystique*. In it she addressed a certain group of women: housewives, women following the path that society, and their own mothers, had told them would bring them the most fulfillment. In research for the book, Friedan interviewed dozens of women who purportedly had found fulfillment in this career. In an early group she interviewed, she found anything but.

> Sixteen out of the twenty-eight were in analysis or analytical psychotherapy. Eighteen were taking tranquilizers; several had tried suicide; and some had been hospitalized for varying periods, for depression or vaguely diagnosed psychotic states. ("You'd be surprised at the number of these happy suburban wives who simply go berserk one night, and run shrieking through the street without any clothes on," said the local doctor, not a psychiatrist, who had been called in, in such emergencies.) Of the women who breastfed their babies, one had continued, desperately, until the child was so undernourished that her doctor intervened by force. Twelve were engaged in extramarital affairs in fact or in fantasy.

Instead of finding satisfaction in what was supposedly the most coveted job a woman could have, one supposedly best suited to her womanly nature, that "feminine mystique," the housewives Friedan interviewed nearly unanimously suffered from "the problem that has no name," a kind of malaise and sense of purposelessness, sometimes wracked by depression or anxiety. But another group of women were thriving: those who used their considerable education and talents to go in to professional, paid work. Friedan's solution to women's oppressive condition was to stop being full-time housewives and start getting truly fulfilling work.

In her 1981 book, *Ain't I a Woman?: Black women and feminism*, the black lesbian feminist bell hooks points out that, when Betty Friedan urged women to reconsider the role of housewife and demanded greater opportunities for women to enter the workforce, Friedan was not speaking for working class women or most women of color. Neither was she speaking for lesbians. Women as a group experience many different forms of injustice, and the sexism they encounter interacts in complex ways with other systems of oppression. bell hooks notes that the feminist movement pretends to speak for all women but was made up of primarily white, middle class women who, because of their narrow perspective, did not represent the needs of poor women and women of color and ended up reinforcing class stereotypes (hooks 1981).

But it may be an overgeneralization to say that second wave feminism was a movement of middle-class white women bored with housework and seeking equality out in the world. Alison Jaggar suggests it was more complicated:

Even though I had been educated in both a school and a college founded only seventy-five years earlier by British feminists, I did not learn the word "feminism" until 1970, during a job interview with an elderly male professor. The absence of this word from my youthful vocabulary shows how quickly and completely First Wave feminism had become, in Sheila Rowbotham's words, hidden from history. However, even if I had known the word "feminism," I'm not sure that I would have seen the women's liberation movement of the late 1960's as a continuation of what I then thought was merely a bourgeois struggle to secure the vote and property rights for married women. My generation—who came to be called Second Wave feminists—was inspired less by Wollstonecraft or Mill than by Marcuse, Memmi, and Fanon, and we took ourselves to be extending and deepening the ongoing struggles for what were then called Third World and Black liberation. Today, white feminists of the Second Wave are often portrayed as having been concerned exclusively with securing abortion rights and women's access to the professions. However, many of us aspired not to equality (with straight, white professional men) but instead to a radically new social order.

We imagined that this would include the abolition of gender, race, and class, which in turn would require the disestablishment of the traditional nuclear family, referred to disparagingly as the "het nuke."

Jaggar went on to write one of the founding texts of second wave theory, *Feminist Politics & Human Nature*, in which she laid out a variety of approaches to questions of ethics and politics, from liberal to Marxist to radical, a great array that has since only become even richer.

Like the first wave, many of the leaders of the second wave of feminism were white women seeking equal rights. But also as in the first wave, other voices emerged, broadening the movement. The second wave came to include women of different identities, ethnicities, and orientations. In addition to calling for equal political rights, they called for greater equality across the board, e.g., in education, the workplace, and at home.

More recent transformations of feminism have resulted in a "Third Wave." Third Wave feminists often critique Second Wave feminism for its lack of attention to the differences among women due to race, ethnicity, class, nationality, religion. But the wave analogy only goes so far. It tends to cover over a multiplicity of political concerns and theoretical views. In addition to concerns about women's equality, there emerged approaches that sought appreciation of women's differences, of matters like reproductive rights, child care, and education, the structure of our society and the content of our culture, the workings of languages and how they shape perceptions and permeate our consciousness. Even with all these many themes, by the late twentieth century there were five key features of the new feminist consciousness. In her 1993 book, *The Creation of Feminist Consciousness*, Gerda Lerner puts these as follows:

> Feminist consciousness consists (1) of the awareness of women that they belong to a subordinate group and that, as members of such a group, they have suffered wrongs; (2) the recognition that their condition of subordination is not natural, but societally determined; (3) the development of a sense of sisterhood; (4) the autonomous definition by women of their goals and strategies for changing their condition; and (5) the development of an alternate vision of the future.

The second, fourth, and fifth of these elements have indeed remained aspects of feminism and feminist consciousness. Feminists have indeed focused to a large extent on the ways that society cultivates women's subordination. Feminists also see that they, not others, are the proper authors for charting a new course. But the first and third of these are considerably more problematic. Are women a distinct group? Are they interested in developing a sense of sisterhood, or commonality, with all other women?

The Category of Women

One of the longest debates in feminist theory and practice has been about who the subject of feminism is. In other words, what is a woman? Can "woman" be defined? If there is a category of woman, what does it include? If feminism, like any social movement, needs a subject, on whose behalf is it acting? Labor unions act on behalf of workers; civil rights movements on behalf of those stripped of rights; and – obviously? — women's movement on behalf of women.

Can all women be treated as one group? Thinking so seems to suggest that women as a group share a common set of features, or that they all suffer the same injustices, and men as a group all reap the same advantages. But of course this is not the case, or at least not straightforwardly so. But even as early as first wave feminism, questions arose about this category of women. As we saw earlier, Sojourner Truth railed against the then common view of "woman" that took white women's experience as paradigmatic. If common experience is what makes women one group, the lack of it makes it hard to pinpoint any such group.

Perhaps there is something about the nature of women themselves that makes women one group? But here too there is trouble. To the extent that feminist theory tries to pinpoint some kind of specific difference between the sexes that can unite women as a group, many have criticized such a move for being essentialist. Essentialism, as we'll see in chapter four, involves identifying distinct qualities that are necessary features of something. Are there certain qualities that are peculiar to women? As soon as anyone starts specifying what might unite women as a group, trouble arises—either the danger of claiming there is some particular necessary quality women have (essentialism) or of mistaking the features of one group of women (say, middle-class white women) for the features of all women.

Such pitfalls are part of a larger set of criticisms that have run through feminist theorizing since the 1970s, with non-white, non-middle-class, and non-western women questioning the very category of "woman," along with the notion that this title could be a boundary-spanning category that could unite women of various walks of life. As we saw with bell hooks' response to Friedan, criticisms of a unitary identity of "woman" have been motivated by worries that much feminist theory has originated from the standpoint of a particular class of women who mistake their own particular standpoint for a universal one. What is so damning about this kind of critique is that it mirrors the one that feminists have leveled against mainstream political theorists who have taken the particular category of men to be a universal category of mankind, a schema that does not in fact include women under the category of mankind but marks them as other.

In many respects, instead of continuing to look for a good definition of "woman" that would apply to all women, for several decades feminists have been moving in the opposite direction, pointing to the proliferation of identities that might fall under the category of women and often calling for more solidarity among those who share an identity narrower than "woman." A good example is the founding statement of the Combahee River Collective's 1982 "A Black Feminist Statement," in which they wrote,

> as children we realized that we were different from boys and that we were treated different—for example, when we were told in the same breath to be quiet both for the sake of being 'ladylike' and to make us less objectionable in the eyes of white people. In the process of consciousness-raising, actually life-sharing, we began to recognize the commonality of our experiences and, from the sharing and growing consciousness, to build a politics that will change our lives and inevitably end our oppression.

Intersectionality

Avant la lettre, the Combahee River Collective was describing a phenomenon now known as intersectionality, that is, being oppressed on more than one dimension and being put in a very unique kind of situation of this intersection. The Collective understood that they faced oppression both for being women and for being black. Feminists find themselves at many other intersections as well, where gender meets color, sexual orientation, sexual identification, class, and religion. For the most part, but not entirely, feminism has come to be a big tent movement, taking seriously the multiple perspectives that arise from these many intersections. While feminism as a whole, I believe, is very capacious, there are particular feminists who have been homophobic or transphobic, anti-Islamic or racist, elitist or classist. I will turn to some of these in due course.

Today feminist theory and practice is more diverse than ever and, for the most part, has a very broad and capacious understanding of the many varieties of women's identities, social locations, and concerns. Feminist theory has also split off into many different kinds of approaches and topics. Feminist theory has a vast literature, book series, journals, scholarly societies, and with them new kinds of disagreements. The questions — what is a woman? And whom does feminism serve? — continue to animate the field, along with a further question, is there a category of woman at all? In the 1990s, the very notion of "the subject" or "the self" came under fire. For a few decades, theory had been taking a new direction, in short, the "linguistic turn," a view that who we are is constructed all the way down. Perhaps the most important feminist text in this direction was Judith Butler's *Gender Trouble*, which I will return to later in this book. Suffice for now it raised the questions of whether the feminist "we" is nothing but a "phantasmatic construction" and the category of woman anything more than a performance.

Even with all of feminism's diversity, there is still something that unites the various strands: a common goal of ridding the world of oppression, domination, and sexism, in whatever form it takes. As bell hooks puts it in her 1989 book, *Talking Back*:

> Feminism, as liberation struggle, must exist apart from and as a part of the larger struggle to eradicate domination in all its forms. We must understand that patriarchal domination shares an ideological foundation with racism and other forms of group oppression, and that there is no hope that it can be eradicated

> while these systems remain intact. This knowledge should consistently inform the direction of feminist theory and practice. (hooks 1989, 22)

On hooks' account, the defining characteristic that distinguishes feminism from other liberation struggles is its concern with sexism:

> Unlike many feminist comrades, I believe women and men must share a common understanding — a basic knowledge of what feminism is — if it is ever to be a powerful mass-based political movement. In *Feminist Theory: From Margin to Center*, I suggest that defining feminism broadly as "a movement to end sexism and sexist oppression" would enable us to have a common political goal... Sharing a common goal does not imply that women and men will not have radically divergent perspectives on how that goal might be reached. (hooks 1989, 23)

In other words, it is not really necessary to have a unified category of women in order to have a feminist politics.

Feminist Theory

I've briefly outlined some of the key moments in the history of feminist movements, times in which women from all walks of life and places in the world entered into the very public sphere from which they had long been barred to claim their own political dignity, agency, and rights. As feminist activists fought these struggles, feminist theorists (many also activists) started thinking through and writing about the prevailing norms and structures. They interrogated how these norms were constructed, what suppositions lay under them, how they were formulated in a way that always seemed to benefit men and generally keep women in their supposed place, whether the bedroom, the nursery, or the kitchen.

Until a few decades ago, one could not go to graduate school to study "feminist philosophy." While students and scholars could turn to the writings of Simone de Beauvoir or look back historically to the writings of "first wave" feminists like Mary Wollstonecraft, most of the philosophers writing in the first decades of the emergence of feminist philosophy brought their particular training and expertise to bear on analyzing issues raised by the women's liberation movement of the 1960s and 1970s, such as abortion, affirmative action, equal opportunity, the institutions of marriage, sexuality, and love. Additionally, feminist philosophical scholarship increasingly focused on the very same types of issues philosophers had been and were dealing with, such as epistemology and philosophy of science, but often with a twist by rethinking the fields from new standpoints.

In order to do this feminist intellectual work, many women worked to gain entrée into the halls of academia. They were met with a lot of opposition and hostility. Women graduate students were repeatedly asked why they should be there rather than a man; they would be overlooked for fellowships and teaching opportunities, taunted, insulted, and demeaned. But still, they persisted. The most hostile disciplines tended to be those that wanted to be most rigorous, including the natural sciences, quantitative social sciences, and the discipline of philosophy. In philosophy, many of the few women who started graduate school in the 1960s were interested in the traditional areas such as metaphysics, epistemology, and ethics, but in the process many bumped into emerging feminist ideas. When she was a graduate student in philosophy in 1969, Alison Jaggar reports, she accepted an invitation to join a reading group to study women's liberation. "I had not the slightest idea what this meant." But in time "the ideas of women's liberation explained many of my internal conflicts generated by the mixed messages I had received when I was younger," including how uncomfortable it was to be in a predominantly male discipline and why it felt awkward to be taller than the average man. "It was indeed liberating to consider that something was wrong with the prevailing norms of gender rather than something was wrong with me."

What we know today as feminist philosophical scholarship emerged in the 1970s as more women began careers in higher education, including philosophy. As they did so, they also began taking up matters from their own experience for philosophical scrutiny. This is one of the most notable features of the academy becoming more open. New areas of inquiry emerge. Whereas previously disciplines run by mostly white men did not take up issues that did not concern mostly white men. But the gradual influx, facing much opposition, of women and people of color into the disciplines of philosophy and social thought, brought new areas of inquiry. In philosophy, feminists raised important questions about some of its foundational assumptions, for example, that philosophy should focus on the human individual and how that person achieves autonomy. Why not the social collective, many feminists asked. And why idealize independence of mind rather than interdependence, others asked. Even among feminists there were a variety of views on these questions. But they generally agreed on the spuriousness of one common philosophical conceit: the ideal of objectivity as basically a "view from nowhere," that the ideal viewer is not situated in any particular place and can see the whole without any bias. This conceit, they found, was actually a male bias founded on the ways that women were assigned to the realm of matter and bodily needs, supposedly freeing up men to "think for themselves."

Along these same lines, feminist thinkers began to theorize sexual identity, gender norms, and reproductive rights using longstanding philosophical tools. One example is the use of the counterfactual, a philosophical device for considering something from the point of view of a situation that is not the case, but could be the case. Judith Jarvis Thomson used this very traditional philosophical tool in 1971 to take up the ethics of abortion, namely abortion opponents' argument that abortion is immoral because a fetus is a person. One way to counter this could be to deny that a fetus is an actual person—and there are lots of good reasons to do so—but for the sake of argument, Thomson granted it. Her counterfactual was to imagine waking up one morning to find that the Society of Music Lovers has strapped a famous violinist with kidney failure to your back in order to make use of your kidneys. If you unplug him from you, he will die. But are you morally obligated to let him stay plugged in to you? Perhaps you might be willing to do so, but it seems rather odd to say that you are *morally obligated* to do so. The counterfactual highlights how letting the violinist stay hooked up to you is a kindness on your part, but hardly something you *must* do. Thomson analogizes this to abortion. Even if one grants that the fetus is a person, that does not mean that a woman is obliged to carry the pregnancy to term. This argument effectively cuts the legs out from under the argument that abortion opponents had levied against abortion: that the fetus is a person. The counterfactual analogy shows that personhood is insufficient. The likely next reason an abortion opponent would invoke is that the woman is responsible for having gotten herself pregnant in the first place, and so she should suffer through the pregnancy whether she likes it or not. But notice that now we are on entirely different philosophical terrain and the opponent is going to need to muster a different set of arguments.

Along with Thomson, this early generation of feminist philosophers were influenced both by actual problems facing women as well as feminist movements in their midst. They used philosophical training, which was anything but feminist, to work through problems facing women and how women had been depicted in the history of philosophy.

Some feminist philosophers stayed within the approach to philosophy that by the 1970s was dominant: "analytic philosophy," which briefly means an approach that aims for logical rigor and clarity. Others found common cause with theorists from other traditions, including communitarians, pragmatists, and continental philosophers, who had also been marginalized from mainstream philosophy and were raising questions similar to the ones that feminist philosophers were asking, often suspicious of the dominant presuppositions about persons, culture, and society.

In addition to these methodological differences, feminist theorists also have a variety of views about the nature of the problem. Some focus on the failures of modern capitalism; others on the failure to value women's traditional practices, including nurturing and care; and yet others to the poisonous holdovers from Eurocentrism and colonialism. To try to address these various problems, some turn to literatures in psychoanalysis, others to phenomenology, and others to logic and conceptual clarity.

But whatever the approach, all treated previous theory with a hermeneutics of suspicion, wondering what sexist presuppositions had made their way into philosophies of science, art, mind, politics, and ethics. And, together, they opened up new areas of inquiry.

Chapter 3

Theorizing Oppression

What is sexism, and how do we know it when we see it? The late philosopher Iris Marion Young, in her book *Justice and the Politics of Difference*, gave a very systematic account of it through the concept of oppression. She noted five aspects (or "faces") of oppression that might befall any social group: exploitation, marginalization, powerlessness, cultural imperialism, and violence. I now turn to these—plus one more, embodied oppression, which Shannon Sullivan has described— to see what light this account sheds on sexism.

According to Marilyn Frye, oppression consists in "an enclosing structure of forces and barriers which tends to the immobilization and reduction of a group or category of people" and are part of a broader system that asymmetrically and unjustly disadvantages one group and benefits another.

We need not assume that those with more power in a society designed these oppressive structures on purpose, nor that they continue to maintain them. The originators of these structures may be long gone, but the structures remain in place out of habit or socialization.

What makes a particular form of oppression sexist? What makes a particular form of oppression sexist seems to be not just that it harms women, but that someone is subject to this form of oppression specifically because she is (or at least appears to be) a woman. Racial oppression harms women, but racial oppression (by itself) doesn't harm them because they are women, it harms them because they are (or appear to be) members of a particular race. The suggestion that sexist oppression consists in oppression to which one is subject by virtue of being or appearing to be a woman provides us at least the beginnings of an analytical tool for distinguishing subordinating structures that happen to affect some or even all women from those that are more specifically sexist. But problems and unclarities remain.

Two strategies for explicating sexist oppression have proven to be problematic. The first is to maintain that there is a form of oppression common to all women. For example, one might interpret Catharine

MacKinnon's work as claiming that to be oppressed as a woman is to be viewed and treated as sexually subordinate, where this claim is grounded in the (alleged) universal fact of the eroticization of male dominance and female submission (MacKinnon 1987; MacKinnon 1989). Although MacKinnon allows that sexual subordination can happen in a myriad of ways, her account is monistic in its attempt to unite the different forms of sexist oppression around a single core account that makes sexual objectification the focus. Although MacKinnon's work provides a powerful resource for analyzing women's subordination, many have argued that it is too narrow, e.g., in some contexts (especially in developing countries) sexist oppression seems to concern more the local division of labor and economic exploitation. Although certainly sexual subordination is a factor in sexist oppression, it requires us to fabricate implausible explanations of social life to suppose that all divisions of labor that exploit women (as women) stem from the "eroticization of dominance and submission." Moreover, it isn't obvious that in order to make sense of sexist oppression we need to seek a single form of oppression common to all women.

A second problematic strategy has been to consider as paradigms those who are oppressed only as women, with the thought that complex cases bringing in additional forms of oppression will obscure what is distinctive of sexist oppression. This strategy would have us focus in the U.S. on White, wealthy, young, beautiful, able-bodied, heterosexual women to determine what oppression, if any, they suffer, with the hope of finding sexism in its "purest" form, unmixed with racism or homophobia, etc. (see Spelman 1988, 52-54). This approach is not only flawed in its exclusion of all but the most elite women in its paradigm, but it assumes that privilege in other areas does not affect the phenomenon under consideration. As Elizabeth Spelman makes the point:

> ... no woman is subject to any form of oppression simply because she is a woman; which forms of oppression she is subject to depend on what "kind" of woman she is. In a world in which a woman might be subject to racism, classism, homophobia, anti-Semitism, if she is not so subject it is because of her race, class, religion, sexual orientation. So it can never be the case that the treatment of a woman has only to do with her gender and nothing to do with her class or race. (Spelman 1988, 52-3)

Other accounts of oppression are designed to allow that oppression takes many forms, and refuse to identify one form as more basic or fundamental than the rest. For example, Iris Young describes five "faces" of oppression: exploitation, marginalization, powerlessness, cultural imperialism, and systematic violence. Sexist or racist oppression, for example, will manifest itself in different ways in different contexts, e.g., in some contexts through systematic violence, in other contexts through economic exploitation.

Exploitation

The first form of oppression is exploitation, which Karl Marx identified as the process by which one group of people appropriates the product of the labor of other people. Forced exploitation is insidious, but "freely" gotten exploitation is a particular genius of capitalism: the worker freely exchanges some labor for a wage, but the product of the labor that the capitalist has paid for is far more valuable than the wage itself. This was Marx's labor theory of value, the key to his understanding of how capitalism works. It is not the individual transactions between workers and owners that makes for exploitation but the fact that the worker has hardly any other alternative, when the overall economy is capitalist. Then exploitation occurs systematically, as, to use Young's words, "a steady process of the transfer of the results of the labor of one social group to the benefit of another." This becomes a structural relation between two social groups: workers and owners.

Back in the 1970s some Marxist feminists tried to use a Marxian analysis to explain women's oppression, but this is not what Young is doing. She is not focusing on their purely economic exploitation.

Feminists have had little difficulty showing that women's oppression consists partly in a systematic and unreciprocated transfer of powers from women to men. Women's oppression consists not merely in an inequality of status, power, and wealth resulting from men's excluding them from privileged activities. The freedom, power, status, and self-realization of men is possible precisely because women work for them.

Young focuses on two forms of sexist exploitation: material and emotional. The first occurs when women do unpaid work in the household that materially supports men's own productive, paid work; and the second is the work that women take on as nurturers and caregivers, providing men with the emotional and sexual satisfaction to flourish in the world. These forms of exploitation become systematic and structural to the extent that women are dependent on men, whether for reasons of money or status. Then, as a group, "women undergo specific forms of gender exploitation in which their energies and power are expended, often unnoticed and unacknowledged, usually to benefit men by releasing them for more important and creative work, enhancing their status or the environment around them, or providing them with sexual or emotional service."

Marginalization

Young's second form of oppression is marginalization, the process by which a group of people is deemed marginal, that is, of no use socially or materially. They could be an economic underclass, or old people, disabled people, or "any whole category of people ... expelled from useful participation is social life." Young focuses primarily on the ways in which certain groups are excluded from the economic benefits of the economy and the effects of this exclusion. For example, for those who are unemployed to get benefits, they have to suffer intrusions into their privacy and loss of respect. This sort of oppression isn't particularly sexist since, today anyway, women as a group are not considered marginal. While they might be marginalized because of some other aspect of their lives, perhaps disability or old age, they are not marginalized, economically anyway, as a group.

But here I would disagree with Young. As a group, women still get paid less than men and are much less represented in certain high-status fields, from politics to physics. In social situations, women are often ignored while their male partners get asked what they do for a living. So I do think women suffer to some extent from this form of oppression as well.

Powerlessness

The third form of oppression that Young discusses is powerlessness, by which she means the power that comes with social and professional status. It is the difference between the middle class and the working class, or white-collar versus blue-collar work, or professional versus menial employment. Those with higher status have that much more freedom to order their own lives, whereas "the powerless lack the authority, status, and sense of self that professionals tend to have." Young notes three aspects of a professional life: (1) the growth through life of one's education and expertise, (2) a great deal of autonomy in one's day-to-day work life as well as one's leisure and cultural activities, and (3) the presumption of respect. By comporting and dressing professionally and by the effects of a great deal of education, professionals signal that they are worthy of being treated with respect. "Professional dress, speech, tastes, demeanor, all connote respectability."

But as I mentioned in discussing marginalization, there is less presumption of respect towards women than men. Young notes that a white man will generally be treated with respect until his working-class identity is revealed, but women are less likely to begin with such a presumption. Rarely is the presumption that she must be a lawyer or doctor or professor, regardless of how she dresses and comports herself.

The default woman is an assistant to those in power, not someone in power herself.

Why is that? In part this is because until recently it has been relatively rare for women to be in the professions. So the lack of presumption of respect is a matter of habit. But the answer also lies partly in what I will discuss in a later chapter, the metaphysics of sex, the overarching views about the nature of reality. One of these features is a mind/body dichotomy, in which man is associated with mind and women with body. Women are often reduced to their bodily parts, not taken seriously as thinkers, derided for being emotional, wracked with hormones, not able to think straight. Instead they are of the body. And in the norms of respectability, where cleanliness is paramount, being of the body is not at all tidy. As Young notes, the key to respectability is decorum, which includes "repression of the body's physicality and expressiveness."

> For women, disabled people, Blacks, Latinos, gay men, lesbians, and others that continue to be marked out as the Other, however, there remains another obstacle to respectability. Even if they successfully exhibit the norms of respectability, their physical presence continues to be marked, something others take note of, and … often evokes unconscious reactions of nervousness or aversion in others. In being

this chained to their bodily being they cannot be fully and un-self-consciously respectable and professional, and they are not so considered. Upon first meeting someone they must "prove" through their professional comportment that they are respectable, and their lives are constantly dogged by such trials, which, though surely not absent from the lives of white men, are less regular.

Hence, the problem of powerlessness is not just a material fact of one's actual profession but how one is perceived and accorded.

Cultural Imperialism

One of the side-effects of a culture in which some have power and others don't is that the values and attributes of the powerful come to be seen as the norm. When Europe started colonizing the rest of the world in the sixteenth century, it imposed its values. Supposedly in the name of civilizing the heathen, it brought European languages, religions, and values. One of the many crimes of colonialism was cultural imperialism. This is what Young calls the fourth face of oppression: cultural imperialism, where a particular culture reigns, portraying itself as the universal. "To experience cultural imperialism means to experience how the dominant meanings of a society render the particular perspective of one's own group invisible at the same time as they mark it out as the Other."

Cultural imperialism may seem to be rather innocuous because it does not in itself involve violence, overt coercion, or exploitation. But it enacts a notion of what the norm should be, often in terms of race, ethnicity, dialects, gender, and ways of comporting oneself. The message is that everyone should be that particular way, and at the same time it telegraphs that those who are not that way are deficient. For those who do not conform to the dominant norms, it exerts a heavy blow against one's sense of self and how others see one: both invisible and Other.

Under a fraternal order, as we'll discuss in the next chapter, the ideals of what it is to be a man come to be the ideals for what it is to be human. This is part of what is at the root of a conundrum that I will take up, how it is that a woman can never be understood to be a good person. Personhood itself has become gendered as male, with women as the other.

Violence

The final form of oppression that Young discusses is violence, not random violence but violence systematically directed at people as members of a particular group. For example, Blacks, gays, trans people and women are subject to systemic violence today on the basis of their group identity.

Any act of violence can be horrific, but what makes it a form of oppression is when it comes to seem unsurprising, even expected: another black man killed at the hands of the police, another woman raped walking home, another transman assaulted outside a bar. No one is shocked to find that another act of violence against any member of these groups was committed.

And with this, strangely, comes the onus placed on the victim to behave properly, for improper behavior might signal that they "deserved it." It was not so long ago that a woman's lacy miniskirt was shown to jurors as evidence that she was "asking for it." In a 1989 rape trial in Florida, the UPI reported, "A jury, saying a 22-year-old woman got what she deserved because she was dressed provocatively, acquitted a Georgia drifter of kidnapping and raping her at knifepoint. 'We all feel she asked for it for the way she was dressed,' jury foreman Roy Diamond said after Wednesday's verdict. 'With that skirt you could see everything she had. She was advertising for sex.'

Or consider the 2014 case of a white police officer putting Eric Garner in a chokehold for allegedly selling untaxed cigarettes. The fact of a black man selling individual cigarettes was offered as evidence of his criminality, making him deserving of the police violence that killed him. The officer got off free.

Not only are women and Blacks victimized but the larger context signals that they should have stayed in their proper place, that their perpetrators were somehow protecting the bounds of acceptable behavior. So violence against members of groups actually serves a larger social aim: to preserve an illegitimate social order. It intersects with cultural imperialism, upholding the values and interests of those in power.

The message is not lost on any of the members of these groups. "Violence is systemic," Young writes, "because it is directed at members of a group simply because they are members of that group. Any woman, for example, has a reason to fear rape." As a result, most any woman will regularly take precautions to protect herself. The possibility of violence shadows her, becoming a fact of her life. Several years ago, an undergraduate at my university made a brilliant video in which he interviewed various students, faculty, and administrators, asking them the same question: What do you do to protect yourself from sexual violence? The women talked about walking in groups, wielding their keys, etc. The men mostly hemmed and hawed saying, well, they had never really thought about that.

Embodied Oppression

To Iris Young's list, I add a sixth form of oppression, which Shannon Sullivan describes at length in her book, *The Physiology of Sexist and Racist Oppression*. I call this embodied oppression. Sullivan documents how sexist and racist oppression inscribes itself in the bodies of the oppressed and their offspring, how racism and sexism can "constitute the body's muscle fibers, chemical production, digestive processes, genomic markers," hormones, cells, and fibers. A sexist and oppressive world shapes the body as much or more than do genes and hormones. Deleterious environments and experiences can have long-lasting physiological consequences on a person's body. These include not just physical toxins but emotional toxins, stressors that can actually change one's cellular structure, leading to increased disease and premature death. Physical and sexual assaults can leave a legacy long after wounds have healed.

Sullivan takes the reader into the esophagus, around the heart, through the pelvis, and out the bowels of the traumatized. She shows how the passage of food into the mouth and down to the wall of the gut is literally a fold of the external world through the body, troubling usual distinctions between inside and outside. Think about it: the lining of the gastrointestinal tract folded within the body is actually a lining between the inside of the body and the outside. Hence, gastrointestinal troubles are, in a sense, physical refusals to introject the world, which Shannon convincingly links to the high prevalence of digestive troubles, such as Irritable Bowel Syndrome, among women who have been sexually abused. A 1990 study found that 44 percent of patients with "gastrointestinal disorders (constipation, diarrhea, and abdominal pain) reported a history of sexual abuse in childhood." In victims of sexual violence: "women's guts often have difficulty digesting and absorbing components of a sexist world that tends to be hostile to them." The body of one who has been sexually traumatized pushes back: "The refusal to digest is a refusal of the world."

In addition to consequences of the oppression one has directly experienced, embodied oppression can afflict those who have not directly experienced trauma, the children and grandchildren of those who suffered, subsequent generations. This could happen directly, such as a mother with high cortisol levels passing on stress hormones during labor that become embodied in that infant. Or it could happen indirectly in what is known as epigenetic transgenerational inheritance. I will skip all the highly technical explanation, but it works something like this: In generation one, some event triggers a change in a gene's expression, perhaps leading to more fear in the face of a certain event coupled with a certain stimulus. Imagine one experiences a terrifying event while at the same time there is the scent of roses in the air. The person links the smell of roses to the terrifying event, and even just that smell can lead to terror later in life. This can change the way a gene linked to smell is expressed. This altered epigenome can be passed to the next generation, who may experience fear when it encounters the stimulus even without the event. So this later generation finds itself suffering from something that befell a previous generation.

The upshot is that a child could inherit the effects of a previous generation's oppressive environment. Sullivan points to "the case of German children whose mothers were pregnant during the Holocaust and American children whose mothers were pregnant during the September 11 World Trade center attacks." She notes that the "German children were more prone to PTSD even though they had no direct experience of the Holocaust," and that is in comparison with American children who themselves had elevated stress levels. The upshot is this: embodied oppression can pass down through generations.

Chapter 4

The Metaphysics of Sex

Now let us take up the logics that divide the world between those who are worthy and those who are not. We can see them at work through most of recorded history. In reading very closely Greek myths, Johann Jakob Bachofen saw how they developed and took root, especially in the move from pre-Hellenic cultures to the classical Greek fraternal order and its glorification of the more spiritual virtues which men exemplified. In discussing the creation of this order, I noted how monotheism excluded women from practices of theological and symbolic activity. The consequences of this have been enormous, for the ideas created during the past 2,500 years have continued to undergird sexism and all its manifestations, including the six faces of oppression we discussed in the previous chapter. The ideas make it seem almost perfectly natural that some particular groups are suitable targets for exploitation, violence, and marginalization.

Against the notion that some people are "naturally" lesser than others, as Gerda Lerner points out, feminists have argued that their condition is not natural but socially determined. That is certainly so, but these ideas cannot be tested and thrown out in the same way that physical speculations can be. They are not easily rebutted and corrected. They shape our very ways of thinking. They are the air that we breathe.

Beneath and alongside the historical developments that rendered women the second sex, there is a powerful mindset, a way of seeing reality, what we might call a metaphysics. Since Aristotle, metaphysics refers to notions that go beyond physics, views about what is "really real," even if we cannot locate these realities empirically. An x-ray machine might identify a broken bone, but it can never find a soul because whether or not human beings have a soul is a metaphysical, not a physical question. We can see what chemicals are firing in the brain, but this thing called mind is harder to analyze. Questions about what kinds of beings we are, at least any of the really interesting questions, are usually the metaphysical ones.

Just because they are immaterial does not mean they are meaningless or unimportant. As meaning-making creatures, we are compelled to give meaning to brute facts, to tell ourselves a story of how things hold together beneath appearances, what the shapes are all about, what the purpose of life is. Before the time of Socrates, this is what philosophers did: they went about trying to offer an account of the ultimate reality of things: Is everything comprised of one thing or many things? Is the world eternal or unchanging? What are the basic structures and what is happenstance? As the theoretical physicist Carlo Rovelli explains, these early inquiries were the origins of physics and other sciences, giving us concepts like the atom. The Milesians of the fifth century BCE theorized, Rovelli writes, that "atoms are indivisible; they are the elementary grains of reality, which cannot be further subdivided, and everything is made of them. They move freely in space, colliding with one another; they hook on to and push and pull one another. Similar atoms attract one another and join."

The atomists of ancient Greece reasoned their way into their theories. "The Milesians had understood that the world can be comprehended using reason," Rovelli writes. "They had become convinced that the variety of natural phenomena must be attributable to something simple and had tried to understand what this something might be." Ultimately, they arrived at "a kind of elementary substance of which everything was made." They made arguments to counter those with a different view of things, those who argued that the overarching principle must be multiplicity and flux.

Clearly these metaphysical speculations of nearly 2,500 years ago proved extraordinarily useful for science today. They provided hypotheses that could later be tested. Exploring matters metaphysical—speculations about the ultimate nature of reality—can be valuable, provided that it is out in the open and explicit about how it is drawing conclusions. Then a debate can go on about the merits of the different arguments. But if they are not brought to light and examined in their own right, they can be smuggled in to other research to skew the results, just taken as fact, assumed rather than argued for. They become normative claims about how something really ought to be.

So, great care should be taken to make any implicit metaphysical claims explicit and then examine how sound they are. This chapter is devoted to the care that feminists have taken in examining the metaphysical suppositions that undergird the fraternal order. As Sally Haslanger and Ásta write, "in a number of different ways feminists are keen to 'unmask' or 'uncover' or 'demythologize' certain aspects of our ordinary (and philosophical) thinking."

Let us look at the various metaphysical assumptions about the sexes and human nature that have undergirded sexism over millennia. They can be divided into these categories: (1) the presumption that men are the paradigmatic human beings; (2) dualistic and hierarchical thinking; (3) the fallacy that there is a feminine essence; and (4) a metaphysics of solids.

Man, the Default Person

Nowhere has the need to unmask spurious metaphysical thinking been more vital than in prevailing views about human nature and the sexes. Up until the twentieth century, most of such metaphysical views went unexamined. For example, what is it to be a "normal" human being, or rather a more developed one? Is it to act out of love or to act out of principle? Is it to value care or to value justice? If one assumes that higher human development means navigating life through logical reasoning more than empathy, then certain judgments will follow. As we'll see in chapter six, in the twentieth century this very phenomenon led some developmental psychologists to conclude that boys develop morally better than girls. These conclusions were based on implicit metaphysical assumptions about what human development should look like, namely that more advanced people and peoples act out of principle and for the sake of justice; lesser developed or more "primitive" peoples are motivated by love and care, acting out of emotion rather than reason. While human beings need to be tended to and nurtured, the supposition goes, ultimately they should "grow up" and act for the sake of universal principles, not particular circumstances.

Feminism faces a central challenge: prevailing views on what it is to be a good person and what it is to be a woman are diametrically opposed. Throughout nearly all the world, for at least the past 2,500 years, up until and including this very moment, it is impossible to use our cultures' ways of thinking to understand that a good woman can be a good person. This is not a philosophical riddle. One can turn on the news and watch a woman running for public office to see the impossible conundrum. If she is ambitious, she has betrayed the ideals of her sex. If she is modest and coy, she is a weak human being and certainly not suitable for public office. In the dominant imaginary, a good person is principled and strong, active and rational, guided by the head rather than the gut or the heart, all qualities that have been admired in men and often derided in women. A good woman is caring and particular, passive and emotional, guided by the heart and not so much the head, all the better to care for others' needs and feelings.

What if a woman decides not to be "a good woman" and instead just simply be a person, that is, what if she decides to eschew all the trappings of womanhood and be neutral without going so far as to eschew gender binaries altogether? Can she opt for neutrality or be what linguists call un-marked? As Deborah Tannen explains,

The term "marked" is a staple of linguistic theory. It refers to the way language alters the base meaning of a word by adding a linguistic particle that has no meaning on its own. The unmarked form of a word carries the meaning that goes without saying -- what you think of when you're not thinking anything special. The unmarked tense of verbs in English is the present -- for example, visit. To indicate past, you mark the verb by adding ed to yield visited. For future, you add a word: will visit. Nouns are presumed to be singular until marked for plural, typically by adding s or es, so visit becomes visits and dish becomes dishes. The unmarked forms of most English words also convey "male." Being male is the unmarked case. Endings like ess and ette mark words as "female."

While attending a small academic conference, Tannen noticed ways in which men's and women's attire was marked or not. "Each of the women at the conference had to make decisions about hair, clothing, makeup and accessories, and each decision carried meaning," Tannen writes. The kind of makeup and hair telegraphed a meaning, whether studious, serious, sexy, or frivolous. But deciding not to wear any makeup also sent a message: "not interested in men." On a woman, any kind of attire, adornment, or lack of it was marked. "The men in our group had made decisions, too, but the range from which they chose was incomparably narrower. Men can choose styles that are marked, but they don't have to," Tannen notes, "and in this group none did. Unlike the women, they had the option of being unmarked." While men can opt for a neutral wardrobe, women, it seems, cannot. Something about the metaphysics of sex makes neutrality unavailable to women.

Moreover, if a woman tries to be simply a good person by rejecting the norms of feminine goodness, she risks her reputation. If she is not good, she seems to have fallen down entirely on her job. The rules, whether explicit or unspoken (depending on the culture), are very specific. The opposite of a good woman is a fallen woman: wanton, lascivious and desirous, dangerous and seductive, a threat to civilization. All the more reason to keep her in place by whatever taboos and strictures needed. The historical record, kept mostly by men, notes a scattered few women rising up in defiance of these strictures—and society rising up against them.

Let us explore the deep structure of the conundrum that a good woman cannot be a good person and vice versa—and why it is so hard to overcome.

- She is born too late; the stereotype of womanhood is always there in advance.
- For a particular woman to be truly herself, she seems to have to escape the idea of what it is to

be a woman. In other words, she seems to be forced to be an exception to her sex. The only way to differentiate herself from the stereotype is seemingly to renounce her own sex. She is applauded (sometimes) for being like a man, never for being herself.

- Her own desire seems to have been captured by masculine desire. Her desire, perhaps largely unconscious, is to be desired by men. The desire of the other (masculine) desire becomes her own. "But what do I really want," she might ask. Can she extricate this internal foreign desire from her own desire? Is there a tenable distinction between the desire of the other and one's own desire when who we are is formed through our social relations?

To make sense of this, I find a useful analogy in the work of Frantz Fanon. In his book *Black Skin, White Masks*, he writes, "However painful it may be for me to accept this conclusion, I am obliged to state it: For the black man there is only one destiny. And it is white." Likewise, I think, the analog for woman could be, "For the woman there is only one destiny, and it is to be man." There are at least two ways to interpret this. (1) We might say that a woman's destiny is to be just as smart or powerful or respected as a man. But the more a woman excels here, the less of a woman she is. In other words, the measure of her progress becomes "man," a point that Catherine MacKinnon beautifully makes, riffing on Protagoras.

Man becomes the measure of women's value. Or (2) her destiny is not her own destiny but men's destiny: to hold and subdue her, to have and use her as the prop on which men's identity is founded. Both can be true, but the latter is more cataclysmic: If the ideal of personhood is in fact founded on an opposition to the stereotype of womanhood, then it would be logically impossible for a woman to be a good person unless we completely reconstruct what personhood can mean. And now it can become clearer how radically transformative a feminist destiny can be: not to prove that women are just as good and deserving as men, but to undo what it has historically meant to be a man at all; and only after that to reconstruct what women and non-binary people are.

Perhaps the most central feature of "the man" that needs reconstruction is its tight and exclusive association with reason. For to be a "man" meant being endowed with reason. From the ancients to the moderns, reason was the hallmark of humanity. But "when the Man of Reason is extolled, philosophers are not talking about idealizations of human beings," Genevieve Lloyd writes. "They are talking about ideals of manhood." The prevailing idea of the centuries, from Plato through the present, is that men had reason and women, along with colonized people, did not, or at least not in the same way. Men's reason could be developed so that they could seek out the true essence of things, but women's minds were too full of passions and emotions to see clearly.

Seventeenth century philosophers such as Descartes and Spinoza created a theory of mind with profound consequences. As Lloyd writes, "Given an already existing situation of sexual inequality, reason— the godlike, the spark of the divine in man—is assigned to the male. The emotions, the imagination, the sensuous are assigned to women. They are to provide comfort, relief, entertainment and solace for the austerity which being a Man of Reason demands."

Consider this more contemporary anecdote. Describing Simone de Beauvoir's childhood relationship with her father Georges, the biographer Deirdre Bair writes (in a chapter titled "The Girl with a Man's Brain"):

> "Simone thinks like a man!" Georges would say, and for years she preened herself whenever she heard these words, considering them the highest compliment he could pay her... She identified herself with her father, not as a man, not wanting to be a man or regretting that she had not been born one, but as a superior woman.

Much of the association of reason with men stemmed from Plato's philosophy which distinguished sense perception from reason, the former deemed inferior. Our senses can deceive us, but the mind can use reason and logic to see the truth of things. Over the centuries this mind/body dichotomy was mapped on to the dichotomy male/female. Women, supposedly tied to their bodies more than men, lacked reason needed to govern themselves and so needed a man to decide matters for them. With the advent of democratic self-rule, that dichotomy and the logic underlying it stayed in place.

Beauvoir notes that "a man never begins by presenting himself as an individual of a certain sex; it goes without saying that he is a man." The default, basically, of being a human being is to be a man. To be a woman is to be a peculiar kind of human being, one with "extra parts," hormones, quirks, unlike men's parts, hormones, and quirks which are taken to be the norm.

It wasn't until the 1990s that the National Institutes of Health stopped the practice of excluding women from clinical trials because of their supposed "extra" hormones and such. As Karen H. Rothenberg writes, "Several notions associated with gender have contributed to the systematic exclusion of women from clinical research. These factors include the perception of men as the 'norm,' the idea that hormonal differences in women will 'complicate' research results and increase costs, the traditional role of women, and the primarily male-dominated research community... Science has a long history of viewing men as the standard by which all things are measured. 'Like the pronoun 'he,' it was taken for granted that the white male subject stood for all of us.' Because the research community views men as the norm, they see differences in women as unknown variables that tend to confound results. For example, women present factors such as menstrual cycles, pregnancy, teratogenic liability, and menopause. Some researchers argue that these factors complicate research and add excess costs to experimentation. Paradoxically, 'scientists seem to be confirming that women's bodies are different and more difficult to study. But then by simply extending their male-drawn conclusions to women, they are implying that-with a few obvious exceptions-women's bodies are the same as men's.' These assumptions have discouraged studies on females and have fostered ignorance concerning the special needs of women."

Dualisms & Hierarchies

When feminist theorists came on the scene and peeked under the curtains to examine the scaffolding on which so many beliefs were founded, what they found can be boiled down to a very stark metaphysical set of binary oppositions which always seem to privilege the masculine over the feminine.

As Hélène Cixous asks in her text, *Sorties*:

"Where is she?"
Activity/passivity
Sun/Moon

Culture/Nature
Day/Night

Father/Mother
Head/Heart
Intelligible/Palpable
Form, convex, step, advance, semen, progress
Matter, concave, ground—where steps are
taken, holding- and dumping-ground.
Man

————————

Woman

Following the question of where "she" is, this
simple, almost poetic, list of contrasting qualities
makes plain the answer. Wherever one looks, "she" is
on the side of passivity, receptivity, nature, heart, and
matter. These softer qualities are coded as feminine;
whereas activity culture, daylight, intelligence, and
progress are coded as masculine. Not only do we
know where she is, we know what is better: to be
reasonable, active, and, frankly, a man. In other words,
these binaries are not co-equal; they are hierarchical.

A few of these hierarchical binaries pertain to a
longstanding mind-body dichotomy, which, as we've
seen, the philosopher Plato made much of. He and his
successor Aristotle spent a great deal of philosophical
energy trying to understand what makes human
beings distinctly human. They saw that human
beings, mere mortals, share many of the passions

and hungers of other animals, but they also have more divine attributes, being able to use reason and mind to discern timeless truths from mathematics to logic and universal qualities. Half animal, half divine, human beings are gregarious animals involved in the ephemeral activities of the world as well as reasoning beings with wisdom or Sophia which allow them to apprehend timeless truths. Plato was most adamant that what set human beings apart was reason and that what gets most in the way of reason is the body and its imperfect sense perceptions.

Though not exactly a proto-feminist, Plato was fairly open-minded about women's capacity to reason. But Aristotle had very distinct views that women were simply passive, material receptacles for man's seed. Men gave form to life, women simply offered up the material of their bodies. Likewise, men had more capacity to reason and women less, making it commonsensical that in the household men should rule over women as well as children and slaves. Aristotle saw men as having a greater capacity than women for moral and political judgment. Several centuries later early Christianity would draw on Plato's ideas, and beginning in the twelfth century AD it began drawing on Aristotle's ideas, folding in the mind/body dichotomy and the ways this dichotomy maps on to men and women.

The dichotomies of head/heart and intelligible/palpable also follow from the mind/body dichotomy, with men seen as more rational and women as more emotional, supposedly because men are less encumbered by their bodies and hormones. Women just can't think or see straight.

In the culture/nature dichotomy, men are seen as the ones who create culture, from the arts to the sciences, whereas women are seen as tied up with matters of the body and nature. Culture is the male realm of freedom; nature the feminine realm of necessity. In the larger world of culture, history is made, but in the material world of nature, especially in the household, nothing new unfolds. And that is women's lot, to tend to the cyclical labors of the household, doing the same things, over and over again.

In themselves, dichotomies may be useful for thinking and ordering the world, but when they become so gendered and hierarchical, they stand in the way of seeing that world. Moreover, the distinctions start to fall apart when pressed, especially the reason/emotion dichotomy, where it turns out that without emotion, reason does not function well. And regarding the culture/nature dichotomy, Gerda Lerner points out that it was women who first fashioned tools and vessels for their work and passed along these skills and knowledge, language and the arts, to their children. In general, the metaphysics of sex denigrate the actual work of passing along knowledge to the next generation and the work of socialization and nurturing, as if people could spring up fully formed without anyone else's assistance.

But never mind such actual facts, the binary oppositions, which are actually hierarchical binaries, are firmly entrenched in our gendered metaphysics of the world.

How did woman come to be the underside, the negation, of ideals of progress, reason, and enlightenment? Which came first: women's oppression or the metaphysical notions of who and what women are? This is a truly chicken-or-egg conundrum. The fact of women's oppression allowed for creating definitions of women that undergird their oppression. Debilitating notions of what women are —whether passive, emotional, weak, irrational— serve to naturalize their subordinate positions in the world.

The philosopher and legal theorist Catherine MacKinnon insists that oppression came first. First came dominance and only afterward came definitions to uphold power inequalities and hierarchies, and construct "social perceptions and reality." In an essay of 1984, MacKinnon writes, rather allegorically,

> Here, on the first day that matters, dominance was achieved, probably by force. By the second day, division along the same lines had to be relatively firmly in place. On the third day, if not sooner, differences were demarcated, together with social systems to exaggerate them in perception and in fact, because the systematically differential

delivery of benefits and deprivations required making no mistake about who was who. Comparatively speaking, man has been resting ever since. Gender might not even code as difference, might not mean distinction epistemologically, were it not for its consequences for social power.

The historical record of patriarchy partially supports MacKinnon's genesis story if we begin that story with people settling down into agricultural communities, then wars of conquest arising, then the exchange of women as objects of property. But that took longer than a metaphorical day. Even so, it was after patriarchal domination was in place that symbolic systems arose that coded women as subordinate to men, where "differences were demarcated" and social systems designed to exaggerate these difference. Men's domination of women preceded gender stereotypes subordinating women. The stereotypes came later but, even though overt domination of women has been largely delegitimized, they persist and serve to perpetuate domination. So even if MacKinnon is right that there was some original moment of domination that was the original cause for women's subordination, which was then supported by gender stereotypes, these stereotypes now continue to keep them oppressed.

Women's "essence"

An ancient metaphysical category is essence, which generally means a particular characteristic of something that makes it what it is. To identify something's essence is to identify what invariable properties it must have to be "what it is." Aristotle relied on this idea to distinguish essential features of something from accidental ones. The essence of a table, for example, would be that it has a surface; whether it is made of wood or metal is inessential, an accidental attribute. If a table changes color, it is still a table; but if it loses its surface and is just a collection of legs, it is no longer a table. Well, that is all fine and good, especially since a man-made item like a table is designed with a purpose, some particular end in mind that its creator, here a carpenter, aims to achieve. But it is a bit more complicated to define the essence of a creature, whether made by nature or God. Something made by nature could have evolved with no particular end in mind. If made by God, then mortals are at a disadvantage to discern God's purpose.

But some tried, most famously St. Thomas Aquinas, saying that women are deficient and misbegotten, naturally subordinate to men, and that their essential value is for "the generation of the species," that is, sexual reproduction. (This is why the Catholic Church disapproves of contraception, the purpose of sex is reproduction, not pleasure. Pleasure, from an Aristotelian point of view, is an "accidental" feature of sex, not an essential one.) In other words, according to Aquinas, a woman's essence is to make babies. Their function is sexual, bodily, and natural. For them, biology is necessity. Men's function and essence, to the contrary, is rational, it is about transcending nature through mind.

In response to that kind of thinking, linking women's biology with their supposed destiny and essence, decades ago feminist theorists started making a strong distinction between biological sex and culturally-constructed gender roles. Beauvoir famously wrote that women are made, not born. By that she meant that the qualities that make someone noticeably a woman or feminine are not natural phenomena but characteristics that come from history and culture. Or, in more contemporary parlance, while biological sex might be a natural phenomenon, genders, such as masculine and feminine, are cultural productions. Today theorists refer to this as the "sex/gender" distinction, though even it has been troubled by the realization (thanks to Judith Butler) that even our understanding of biological sex is refracted through a cultural imaginary.

The main insight here is that, contrary to an old view that, for females, anatomy is destiny, feminist theorists have for decades pointed out that biological differences between the sexes cannot provide a full account of the stereotypes and prejudices that have rendered women the second sex, always less than, inferior to, or the negative image of man. These theorists have wanted to bracket away biological matters and focus on sexist stereotypes. So they take "male" and "female" to refer to biological sex and "man" and "woman," as well as "masculine" and "feminine," to refer to gender. This sex/gender distinction means a number of things. One is that there is a disjunct between what our culture understands a woman to be and what the facts of her biology are. In other words, biology is not destiny. Another is that gender stereotypes can float among bodies, such that a biological female might code as masculine or a male body present itself as feminine. A third implication is that gender stereotypes can be transformed. If they were culturally constructed, they can be reconstructed; so we need not be trapped in endlessly repeating sexist assumptions about bodies. According to this sex/gender distinction, whatever biological differences there are between the sexes do not justify sexist stereotypes and so it is illegitimate to assign an essence to a woman based on biology.

The sex/gender distinction has been central to feminist philosophy, but even here many variations on the theme flourish. Where analytic feminism, which is very critical of essentialism, holds the sex/gender distinction practically as an article of faith, Continental feminists tend to suspect either (1) that, following the early work of Judith Butler, the meaning of the supposedly purely biological category of sex is itself socially constituted or (2) that, where the sex/gender distinction tends to dismiss sexual difference as a cultural artifact, it actually needs to be thought through more.

In her book, *Essentially Speaking*, Diana Fuss takes this latter route. She acknowledges the value of the sex/gender distinction, explaining that in "feminist theory, the idea that men and women, for example, are identified as such on the basis of transhistorical, eternal, immutable essences has been unequivocally rejected by many anti-essentialist feminists concerned with resisting any attempts to naturalize human nature." But Fuss shares the concerns of the Belgian feminist, Luce Irigaray, that women are not just made by the social order, they can make themselves. "How can I say it?" Irigaray asks. "That we are women from the start. That we don't have to be turned into women by them, labeled by them, made holy and profane by them. That has always already happened, without their efforts." Irigaray takes women's biology, namely the fact that women have two sets of lips, that "speak together" and provide pleasure, as starting points for thinking about what women are. After she published her early books laying out these ideas (*Speculum of the Other Woman* and *This Sex Which is Not One*), many feminist theorists called Irigaray out as being an essentialist.

Fuss defends Irigaray's strategy, which is similar to Beauvoir's. Beauvoir cites the anthropologist Levi-Strauss's observation that human beings generally tend toward viewing "biological relations as a series of contrasts; duality, alternation, opposition, and symmetry." Males become sovereign by proclaiming themselves in opposition to the Other, woman. As Beauvoir puts it, while woman "is called, 'the sex,' by which is meant that she appears essentially to the male as a sexual being," in fact she is really seen as "the incidental, the inessential as opposed to the essential. He is the Subject, he is the Absolute—she is the Other." In other words, the fraternal order has not really identified women's essence as merely biological sex; the fraternal order doesn't really assign women any essence at all. As Fuss puts it, in the history of philosophy, particularly in Aristotle, "woman is asserted to have an essence [weak, passive, receptive, emotional] which defines her as woman and yet, on the other hand, woman is relegated to the status of matter and can have no access to essence." This is because in Aristotle's metaphysics, in order to realize one's essence one must be active, one must turn what is merely potential into its actuality. But women are denied having any capacity to actualize their potential. So, as Fuss notes, the central contradiction running through patriarchal thought is this: "woman has an essence and it is matter" without any capacity to actualize its potential, so, "put slightly differently, it is the essence of women to have no essence."

If we take seriously the view that the fraternal order renders women as inessential, as merely the negation or man, a way for him to hold her up as his mirror to point to his own positive attributes— after all, it is the possibility of being emasculated, feminized, in any way "like a girl," that clarifies what it is to be a man—then the task for feminist philosophy could be to locate women's essence, what they *really* are. This second view goes looking for what women might be positively, not as inessential but as having their own specificity. Here the task is to go in search of what women's real essence might be. Where the sex/gender distinction focuses on criticizing how sexual difference has been constructed, this other one focuses on uncovering real sexual difference.

Those who take this "difference feminism" approach go in two different directions, first there is the maternalist and ethics-of-care views. We saw a glimpse of the maternalist view in the histories that tried to uncover a matriarchal history, based on all the positive virtues of mothering. The second direction that difference feminism takes is toward theories of sexual difference, many informed by contemporary engagements in psychoanalytic literature. We will touch on both of these in chapter six.

Metaphysics of Solids

Part of the metaphysics of sex is what, following Irigaray, we can call a metaphysics of solids, taking particular physical attributes to be better than other attributes, namely that what is solid and firm is better than what is fluid and malleable. Perhaps it is a testament to the limits of human imagination, but too often someone's physical characteristics are taken to be their psychological characteristics as well. This is surely the case with the sexes. The physical characteristics of the human male, from muscles to the male sexual organ, are, at least ideally, hard, taut, powerful, and firm. And, by extension, in our limited imagination, a good man will have the same psychological characteristics. A good man isn't flabby or wishy-washy; he is principled, firm, and strong.

And a good woman seems to be the opposite: supple, tender, soft, pliable, not just physically but psychologically. Feminine women, as the stereotype goes, do not frequent the weight room in a gym; they do cardio, Pilates, and yoga. They don't aim to build muscle, rather they aim to take up as little space as possible. Many straight women want male partners who are bigger and taller, the better to show in contrast their own diminutive femininity.

Femininity and masculinity are not separate but equal ideals. Femininity is not the equal counterpart to masculinity. It is, as the philosopher Luce Irigaray argues, an imaginary that props up masculinity. In fact, as we have seen, femininity doesn't even have any real content. It is simply the negative of the ideal of Man. A good man is principled, firm, and strong only in *contrast* to the feminine. I'll come back to this in a moment, but first let's pause on how these ideals of masculinity and femininity are what we can call "imaginaries," however tethered they might be to physical reality.

An imaginary is a largely unconscious or pre-conscious mental image of what things are like, what they "really" are. I am using this term "imaginary" somewhat the same as the word "metaphysics," though this latter term aims to capture the real truth of the matter. An imaginary, by contrast, might have no truth at all on its side. But it has a lot of power. A prevailing imaginary construct, however unreal, gets its power and reality to the extent that it is widely shared and believed. For example, the more people believe that the ideal person is principled and strong, the more firmly rooted that imaginary becomes. Irigaray's most important observation is that the reigning sexual imaginaries are masculine ones, tethered to the male body, created by and to the benefit of men, even if there is no one left in the world who plotted to set up this schema. In fact, even those who are harmed by the schema can believe it with all their hearts. Hence the women who long for a taller partner with muscles firmer than their own, with a bigger paycheck, and more social status. But even if she is not that conventional, even if she frequents the weight room, she might be a tad embarrassed by her biceps.

Even into the twentieth century, Irigaray notes, the prevailing theoretical schemas still succumb to this masculinist imaginary. As Dorothea Olkowski puts it in her essay, "Body, Knowledge and Becoming-Woman: Morpho-logic in Deleuze and Irigaray," Irigaray's "persistence, her will to 'poke around' in systems which no one has previously approached in this manner, produces the reality of those philosophical systems. They are, she discovers, systems of thought dominated by the logic and linguistics of male sexual organs." These systems of thought include those of the leading psychoanalytic thinkers, Sigmund Freud and Jacques Lacan. Freud famously built his theory largely around the boy child's fear of castration, his willingness to submit to social taboos against incest so that no one lops off his pet organ. And as for girls, as soon as they discern that boys have something that they lack, supposedly, they develop penis envy. Lacan picked up on this focus on the penis and elevated it to a new symbolic status: the Phallus, which is really the symbol of what the penis affords: power, completion, plenitude, even if no one with a dick ever really gets what it promises. In Lacan's work, the search for what the Phallus promises becomes the motor engine of desire and life. Now, I know that this all sounds somewhat implausible, but it is true that in a world where men have power and men have dicks, then the Dick would become a symbol of power. So I do see that Freud and Lacan were actually on to something when describing, empirically, penis envy and the castration complex.

But Irigaray takes them to task for something else, for failing to see how femininity is constructed *according to* the masculine imaginary—though I think she fails to see that Freud and Lacan were in on the joke. (In his lectures on anxiety, Lacan pokes fun at the organ which "is never likely to hold up very far on the road along which jouissance does its bidding.") In any case, Irigaray's major point is correct: In the prevailing imaginary, femininity itself has no essence; it is flabby and soft and simply passive. Really, it is not even that. Femininity is a mirror held up to the man for him to gaze adoringly at his own self, the mirror reverse of her. A woman "serves (only) as a *projective map*," Irigaray writes, "for the purpose of guaranteeing the totality of the system." She is only a geometric prop, thanks to her 'fluid' character, which has deprived her of all possibility of identity with herself within such a logic."

What Irigaray is describing is reflected in the everyday terms people use to contrast masculinity and femininity, the former being firm, decisive, and perhaps a bit rigid; the latter being soft, unsure, and fluid. In an essay on "the 'mechanics' of fluids," Irigaray explores—in her famously difficult language— the "fluid" character of femininity. This is how the prevailing metaphysics of solids positions women, as a place with no place, with nothing at all. But in reality, Irigaray argues, women are more than all that.

I will come back to this later in the book. For now my aim is to highlight the metaphysical imaginaries that undergird sexism and eclipse women's actual desires. As Irigaray puts it, "The more or less exclusive—and highly anxious—attention paid to erection in Western sexuality proves to what extent the imaginary that governs it is foreign to the feminine.

For the most part, this sexuality offers nothing but imperatives dictated by male rivalry: the 'strongest' being the one who has the best 'hard-on,' the longest, the biggest, the stiffest penis."

Masculine Imaginaries

In this imaginary, just as a penis is at its best when it is hard, a person is as well. And since, as we saw earlier, the supposed default subjectivity is male, then the hard and firm character is the best one; the soft and fluid the least. This is not just the case of the metaphysics of sex but, as Olkowski points out, the metaphysics of knowledge itself, which, in man's image, is based on a logic of solids and eschews as meaningless anything fluid, which is associated with women. The reigning masculine metaphysics of solids can hardly bear an alternative. As Irigaray puts it, "Thus if every psychic economy is organized around the phallus (or Phallus), we may ask what this primacy owes to a teleology of reabsorption of fluid in a solidified form. The lapses of the penis do not contradict this: the penis would only be the empirical representative of a model of ideal functioning; all desire would tend toward being or having this ideal."

In this sexual imaginary, Irigaray writes, woman "is only a more or less obliging prop for the enactment of man's fantasies." She is just a "hole" for his pleasure. In what Irigaray refers to as this phallomorphic imaginary, men's pleasure takes center stage with women being there to serve it. "That she may find pleasure there in that role, by proxy, is possible, even certain. But such pleasure is above all a masochistic prostitution of her body to a desire that is not her own." Moreover, it leaves her "not knowing what she wants, ready for anything, even asking for more." In the millennia-long reign of the phallomorphic imaginary, "woman's desire has doubtless been submerged by the logic that has dominated the West since the time of the Greeks." One would need to dig "beneath the traces of this civilization" to the "vestiges of a more archaic civilization that might give some clue to woman's sexuality," to women's own desire.

Chapter 5

Feminist Desire

Now that we have surveyed the origins and central features of a world that is bent on subordinating women, it is time for asking: What do feminists call for doing? What do women want? And, as we'll turn to in the next chapter, how do they suggest that we live differently? In short, what is to be done? At the very least we know this: the answers to these questions should be given by women themselves. That is a central feature of feminist consciousness. Recall what Gerda Lerner had noted: feminist consciousness calls for "the autonomous definition by women of their goals and strategies for changing their condition." In other words, change should be driven by women's desires, their *autonomous* desires. Instead of others governing what they do, women should be able to govern themselves. They should be able to identify and pursue their own desires.

But being able to identify and pursue their own desires begs the questions of what is one's own desire, whether there is a self that is not so shaped by its culture that it can peel away culture sufficiently to see its own desire. What if, as Mari Ruti asks in her book with the lovely title, *Penis Envy and Other Bad Feelings*, "women have been taught to eroticize—and therefore find pleasure—in their subordination"? And what does it mean to ascertain one's desires autonomously when autonomy itself has been a hegemonic feature of the "democratic" regime of the brothers? To address these questions, this chapter has two sections: one on the nature/culture dichotomy and a second on feminist interpretations of autonomy.

Nature or Culture?

As I mentioned earlier in chapter two, in the late twentieth century much social theory took the linguistic turn, turning to studying language itself to understand how it mediated between people and the world. This turn happened across many very different fields, from analytic philosophy (including the

Vienna School and ordinary language philosophy) to continental philosophy, most famously Lacanian psychoanalysis and deconstruction. In these latter domains, a common view came to be that language and the larger symbolic realm structures human subjectivity all the way down, that there is no "true" kernel of the self that can be accessed, because once we have become speaking beings all our consciousness is refracted through language. This would mean that even who we think we are is linguistically mediated and perhaps thoroughly constructed through our social environment and our linguistic symbols, we are, in short, made, not born. We can call this a constructivist account and oppose it to an account that would hold, to the contrary, that something innate to the self remains in place. This could be something like a person's basic temperament or constitution.

The conundrum is this: if women are thoroughly made in the image of what the socio-symbolic system thinks they should be, then how could they ever resist? Could they peel away what the system says they should want enough to discern what they really want? And is there any "true self" there at all? These were the kinds of questions that feminist and other social theorists were asking at the end of the twentieth century, with dozens of edited volumes published with titles like, *Who Comes After the Subject?* Let's look at how this played out in feminist theory and then what followed.

Trouble with the Sex/Gender Distinction

In her groundbreaking book of 1990, *Gender Trouble*, Judith Butler follows the linguistic turn to question the sex/gender distinction which, as discussed in chapter four, was supposed to differentiate between natural bodies (sex) and socially constructed genders. Hence in the sex/gender distinction of female/woman, the former is considered natural and the latter socially/linguistically constituted. Against this view, Butler argued that even sex terms like female and male were socially mediated. "If the immutable character of sex is contested, perhaps this construct called 'sex' is as culturally constructed as gender; indeed, perhaps it was always already gender, with the consequence that the distinction between sex and gender turns out to be no distinction at all." The way we use these terms *female* and *male* is refracted through cultural, linguistic constructions.

> Cultural assumptions regarding the relative status of men and women and the binary relation of gender itself frame and focus the research into sex-determination. The task of distinguishing sex from gender becomes all the more difficult once we understand that gendered meanings frame the hypothesis and the reasoning of those biomedical inquiries that seek to establish "sex" for us as it is prior to the cultural meanings that it acquires. (109)

But while Butler argues that *both* sides of the sex/ gender distinction are constructed, that even sex is gender, she also notes that in living out the norms we've been subjected to we are also performing and possibly transforming them in the course of our lives. Yet it is hard to locate the source of this agency for language continues to shape our thinking except where "the culturally enmired subjects negotiates its construction," as she says in the conclusion of *Gender Trouble.*

Along with Butler's continentally-informed reading, analytic feminist philosophers of science have also pointed out that implicit values can make their way into interpretations of physical phenomena. As Sara Weaver and Carla Fehr wryly observe in their contribution to *The Routledge Companion to Feminist Philosophy*, "cultural beliefs about gender" can be so powerful that they make their way into observations of even plants and cells. Take algae, which one Victorian scientist claimed were differentiated between the active male ones and the passive and hence, obviously, female ones. "The problem is that algae do not actually have sexes in the way that many other organisms do. The 'males' that he is describing do not have sperm, testes, or XY chromosomes," Weaver and Fehr write. "They are only male" insofar as this scientist decided that "that which is active is male and that which is passive is female." In other words, metaphysical assumptions about gender make their way into interpretations of supposedly purely natural phenomena.

Weaver and Fehr note two main problems underlying an array of biological research: first the influence that gender stereotypes have in framing research questions and interpreting results, second the way that essentialist and determinist models "promote ideas of inherent and fixed differences between men and women." These models assume that "males and females belong to natural categories much like gold and silver do" and that one can zero in on the specific features or characteristics that separate one group from the other. For example, essentialist and determinist models take certain low-level biological phenomena, such as hormones and genes, to be the essence and destiny of one's being; they allow scientists to extrapolate from men having more testosterone to claim that they are more inherently more competitive than women, whereas women's estrogen levels make them more nurturing.

Weaver and Fehr do not draw from their findings that the sex/gender distinction itself is in trouble, but they do see the kind of trouble it gets into. This happens when cultural stereotypes start infecting scientific thinking such that it seems perfectly "natural" that the more active algae would be male. What comes to appear as natural is an effect of cultural constructions.

Gender Dissatisfaction

Much continental feminist philosophy has followed Butler's constructivist path, holding broadly that no one can know the world as it really is but only how it is culturally and linguistically represented. A favorite mantra of the 1990s was, translated from French, "there is nothing outside the text." Another was that everything is in "the house of language." A few decades earlier, Jacques Lacan had acknowledged that there was a Real, but once we enter into language we lose direct access to it.

Eventually the pendulum swung the other way, from the power of the socio-symbolic order to subject us and "normalize" us to the resistance of the material real. This alternative now goes by the name "new materialism." According to Claire Colebrook, in her contribution to *The Routledge Companion to Feminist Philosophy*, new materialism does not just take up the body side of the mind/body or form/ matter dichotomies, it attempts to show how much bodies and materiality can resist normalization, how they can really have a life of their own. Along these lines, Colebrook gives another account of what Luce Irigaray is up to, namely that she was stressing "the materiality of sexual *difference*, meaning not the biological fixity of two sexes but the process and relations through which the complexity of matter generates ... ways of forming oneself in relation to the world."

Somewhat aligned with new materialism is a new feminist focus on phenomenology, going by the name "critical phenomenology." Like new materialism, but maybe not to the same degree, it rejects philosophy's long and exclusive focus on psyche and mind and its tendency to ignore lived experience. Where traditional phenomenology focused singularly on consciousness, critical phenomenology attends more to the body and the experience of embodiment, particularly to the experiences of oppression we considered in chapter three. Embodiment becomes paramount, psyche less so.

Where constructivist accounts have difficulty pinpointing how the psyche can resist the normalizing force of gender and other norms, those movements that turn to the body unfortunately have little to say about the psyche's ability to resist normalization. Fortunately, there is a new type of philosophizing on the scene that is helping think through this problem. It is trans philosophy, which is dissatisfied with both the constructivist (linguistic turn) account and the new materialist account. What is going on when a person born in a biologically male body and born into a rigidly gender-binary world says no to all that? From where come the resources to resist both the biology of one's given body and the subjectivating forces of the socio-symbolic world?

In her contribution to *The Routledge Companion to Feminist Philosophy*, Talia Mae Bettcher points to the limits of the constructivist account: namely where a trans woman who had grown up being thoroughly conditioned to be a man announces, no, I am really a woman. How did her gender dissatisfaction with being assigned male arise if everything gender is not born but made? And if materiality is all that matters, how does the trans woman call for a life that feels very different from one afforded by the body she was born in? To even ask such questions, there must be agency that is neither merely the product of social construction nor something residing in the body. In other words, philosophy needs to find a way to understand the person, that totality of mind, body, circumstances, and temperament, as capable of charting her own life through a maze of conflicting demands.

In a different context, the psychoanalyst and philosopher Joel Whitebook, in an essay in *Debating Critical Theory*, takes up the same question. To those who want to say that all subjectivity is socially constructed, what are we to make of the "constitutional factor" that resists conformism? Whitebook takes seriously both sides, one's native constitution and the force that society exerts in shaping us into some other image. Like the child thoroughly dissatisfied with the gender society has assigned it, any of us can bristle and resist the norms that the fraternal order has assigned.

Psychoanalysis and Desire

Following Bettcher and Whitebook, I believe it is still possible to begin to identify "one's own" desires in the midst of social influences and pressures. Here Freud can help, especially in the account he gives of femininity. "Throughout history people have knocked their heads against the riddle of the nature of femininity," Freud wrote in 1933. "Nor will *you* have escaped worrying over this problem—those of you who are men; to those of you who are women this will not apply—you are yourselves the problem." The reader can imagine that many feminists have taken great umbrage at these words, being told that women are the problem. But Freud can be forgiven on two counts, one is that he was a man and had a hard time understanding what he elsewhere called "the dark continent" of women's desire; the other is that he was trying to unpack something that is really a riddle. Where some feminists see him as having a very backward view of women, others like myself see him as trying to understand "what women want" at that very juncture between the social forces of normalization and the psychic forces of resistance. Are women more passive sexually, and in other areas of life, because that is their nature? Or are they more passive because culture teaches them to be so? Are they able to find a pleasure that is their own?

Biology is of little help, Freud notes, in unpacking the riddle because men and women each have a mixture of sexual traits. But perhaps psychology can help: "We are accustomed to employ 'masculine' and 'feminine' as mental qualities as well, and have in the same way transferred the notion of bisexuality to mental life," Freud writes, well before feminists came up with the sex/gender distinction. "Thus we speak of a person, whether male or female, as behaving in a masculine way in one connection and in a feminine way in another. But you will soon perceive that this is only giving way to anatomy or to convention. You cannot give the concepts of 'masculine' and 'feminine' *any* new connotation." Freud is pointing to the same phenomenon we considered in chapter four: how our metaphysical imaginaries shape our understanding of the sexes. "When you say 'masculine'," Freud writes, "you usually mean 'active', and when you say 'feminine', you usually mean 'passive'."

> One might consider characterizing femininity psychologically as giving preference to passive aims. This is not, of course, the same thing as passivity; to achieve a passive aim may call for a large amount of activity. It is perhaps the case that in a woman, on the basis of her share in the sexual function, a preference for passive behaviour and passive aims

is carried over into her life to a greater or lesser extent, in proportion to the limits, restricted or far-reaching, within which her sexual life thus serves as a model. But we must beware in this of underestimating the influence of social customs, which similarly force women into passive situations. All this is still far from being cleared up. There is one particularly constant relation between femininity and instinctual life which we do not want to overlook. The suppression of women's aggressiveness which is prescribed for them constitutionally and imposed on them socially favours the development of powerful masochistic impulses, which succeed, as we know, in binding erotically the destructive trends which have been diverted inwards. Thus masochism, as people say, is truly feminine.

Freud's point is that neither biology nor an analysis of mental qualities will tell us anything about anyone's essence. As he puts it, "psycho-analysis does not try to describe what a woman is—that would be a task it could scarcely perform—but sets about enquiring how she comes into being." This sounds a bit like Simone de Beauvoir, though Freud's point is somewhat different. He does think that men and women do have a particular nature at birth, one that they share. Babies are born, as he puts it, "polymorphously perverse." They will get pleasure anywhere, and they have no original inclination to love one sex over another. It so happens that the primary caregiver is usually female, so that will be the first love. But immediately as it enters the world social forces go to work to try to turn little boys into heterosexual woman-seeking beings and little girls into heterosexual man-seeking beings. Freud finishes the thought above about "how a woman develops out of a child with a bisexual disposition."

The route for a child to becoming a man or woman, according to Freud, passes through the Oedipus Complex, where the child is faced with giving up its primary attachment to the mother in order to enter into other social arrangements. The boy's path is relatively straightforward: he will give her up now in exchange for the promise of having another woman later. He does not have to give up his budding heterosexuality. For the girl, Freud notes, it is much more complicated. She not only has to give up her desire for her mother, she must also change her own desire from homosexual to heterosexual.

Resisting Subjection

Freud's discussion is marked by many aspersions about female genital pleasure (the clitoris is just a little penis whose pleasure must be renounced), but his larger questions are still pressing. Namely, to what extent is one's sexual desire really one's own or what society has inculcated in one? How malleable are sexual identity and sexual orientation? Is women's supposed passivity or femininity a product of having to renounce homosexual or—let's just say—*queer* pleasure?

The main legacy of Freud's work is that the human being is always in a space of conflict: between psyche and society, between biological drives and psychological instincts, between pleasure and reality. There is no solution to the nature versus culture debate about who we are and how we come to be. We are always both, doomed to be repressed and somewhat miserable from the demands culture places on us, but never willing to give in, always finding some way or another to resist. The resistance might show up as a neurotic symptom—or it might show up as an attempt to change the world.

Autonomy

So far in this chapter I have attempted to show that there is a capacity in the self to resist the demands of culture enough to find one's own desire. Now I turn to this chapter's second task: to explore what it means to act autonomously in a way that does not fall prey to debilitating enlightenment ideals of the band of brothers.

The word *autonomy* has many resonances. Most simply it means something decided on one's own, not being unduly influenced by anyone else. In philosophy it has a far greater resonance, pulling the reader back into the work of the eighteenth century philosopher, Immanuel Kant, whose work revolved around three central questions: (1) what can we know, (2) what shall we do, and (3) for what should we hope. Respectively these pointed to the domains of epistemology, morality, and aesthetics. It is the second one that concerns us here. In deciding what one should do, Kant's main claim is that this should be arrived at autonomously. By this he means on the basis of what one's own reason arrives at, and definitely not heteronomously, that is, not on the basis of anything other than one's own reason.

What might be other than one's own reason? It might be the influence of other people, or it might be the influence of one's own passions. An alcoholic who pours another drink is acting from powerful desire, not reason. The motive is hypothetical, not categorical, meaning the motive is for some particular outcome (here, so I feel better) and not what would be good categorically, that is, good for all under any circumstances. One would never say that the alcoholic was deciding autonomously to have that drink. One can ascertain that one is deciding autonomously if the decision that results is something that admits of no exceptions, when it can be universalized, when it treats all others and one's self as having dignity, that is, infinite worth. If, to the contrary, one is making an exception, for example, that I can cheat just this instance on something, then likely a passion has snuck in.

Lerner the historian was likely thinking of the more mundane meaning of autonomy, believing that women should decide on their own what to do and not on the basis of societal expectations, certainly not on the basis of what their fathers or husbands wanted. But as we've seen, it is not so easy to disregard the Kantian definition, for it is notoriously difficult to peel away societal (heteronomous) expectations from one's "very own," especially since who we are is to a large extent a product of our particular circumstances, history, and culture.

The Trouble with Autonomy

For feminism, autonomy is a mixed bag. The positive side, assuredly, is that it is an ideal of self-governance, and that is a powerful ideal for those who for millennia have been denied it. The freedom and ability to think and decide for oneself has been a central aspect of all attempts at democratization, starting with the ancient

Athenian citizenry through the Enlightenment, and continuing with liberation struggles in the nineteenth and on into the present century.

But on the other side, the ideal of autonomy comes with suppositions that are troubling for feminists: a valorization of the individual over the social, of independence over interdependence, and of reason over the emotions. All these suppositions are wrapped up together. First, the Kantian ideal of autonomy privileges the individual over the social by focusing on the need for the person to decide alone, without any influence from anyone else. The only way to protect an individual's reason, this view goes, is to wall it off from the concerns of other people. So the ideal of autonomy is very individualistic, perhaps even atomistic.

Second, the traditional notion of autonomy puts a high value on independence. Cynthia Willett finds this at work in Freud's iconic discussion of his grandson's mastery of his mother's absence. Freud noted that, when the mother was gone, the boy played a game he had invented of "fort-da" or "gone away, here it is." He took a spool of thread and repeatedly threw it over the side of his crib and then pulled it back again. Freud gathered that this was a repetition of the mother's loss followed by retrieval, a way to master the loss. Willett sees this as involving, for the boy, a denial of his mother's importance. In her book, *The Soul of Justice*, Willett comments on this, "Male selfhood is defined by a problematic response to the contingency and complexity of human interactions, beginning with the boy's stoic response to the mother's power." Instead of tarrying with his need for her or with his loss, the boy tries to rise above it. "From this stoic denial of emotional investment in a relationship with the mother, the boy turns his attention to games of mastery [drawing in the spool]... and episodes of violent destruction [throwing it back out again]." The boy was learning to be a man "by playing games of control," Willett notes, whereas girls do better by immersing themselves in their loss. Willett calls for the need to regenerate male identity through recognizing rather than disavowing the mother's power.

Third, the ideal of autonomy, especially in the Kantian version, disparages emotion, seeing it as getting in the way of reason. This flows from one of the hierarchical binaries we considered in chapter four: intelligible/palpable, which was Cixous' way of putting the reason/passion dichotomy. And all these map on to a mind/body dichotomy. Supposedly, emotions drag us down to biological and hormonal demands, whereas reason can lift us away from these mundane things and allow us to see things more clearly and distinctly (that was Descartes' criteria). In this view, then, to act for oneself, to be autonomous, calls for becoming inured against the pull of love, solidarity, kinship, and longing. After all, supposedly, those are passions that pull on women, not men of reason.

Autonomy in a Feminist Key

While feminists have been very critical of this Enlightenment ideal of autonomy, they have also seen its value, at least if it is in some way reconstructed so that it isn't used to denigrate women and women's concerns. Some feminist philosophers have looked for a "relational" approach, one that would not require self-sufficiency. As Natalie Stoljar explains in her entry on feminist perspectives on autonomy in the *Stanford Encyclopedia of Philosophy*, "If relationships of care and interdependence are valuable and morally significant, then any theory of autonomy must be 'relational' in the sense that it must acknowledge that autonomy is compatible with the agent standing in and valuing significant family and other social relationships. 'Relational' may also deny the metaphysical notion of atomistic personhood, emphasizing instead that persons are socially and historically embedded, not metaphysically isolated, and shaped by factors such as race and class. It is this latter sense of "relational" that will be employed in the following sketch of relational accounts."

The theories Stoljar lays out also try to account for how gender oppression can lead to what looks like failures of autonomy. Take the "deferential wife" who organizes her life around what her husband wants. She cooks what he wants, dresses in a way that pleases him, and in general aims to satisfy his wishes. Is she autonomous or not? Perhaps she is acting rationally, having calculated what it takes to make it in a man's world. To this Stoljar raises Susan Babbitt's objection, that making one's desires subordinate to others is incompatible with autonomy, so, no, she is not acting autonomously. Well, what if she has internalized her husband's and her society's expectations such that they have become her own? Then might one say that the deferential wife is acting autonomously? To the extent that her desire was adapted under circumstances of oppression, this would also not be deemed autonomous.

The feminist theories of autonomy that Stoljar surveys offer a variety of accounts of how oppression impinges on agents' autonomy. While they do not agree, they all come down to the question of how much of the person's agency is really and manifestly *her own*. The more oppressive the circumstances are, the more they undermine agents' autonomy.

There is another school of thought I find quite compelling, one that draws from psychoanalytic social theory. The feminist philosopher and legal theorist, Drucilla Cornell, has worked in this vein and offers a robust feminist account of autonomy, both in a number of her books and in a short but rich essay, "Autonomy Re-Imagined." Recall that the idea of dignity is utterly central to Kant's idea of autonomy. With it he means that individuals have an infinite worth that cannot be traded away for particular gains; and so any moral law must respect everyone as able to choose their own ends. Cornell extends this idea from the individual to family and kinship relationship, by doing so then the dignity of human relationships and networks becomes paramount.

Recall that Kant treated emotions and passions as possibly dangerous to autonomous choice. Reason not the desires should rule. Cornell modifies this view to seeing that deciding one's own ends is not limited to pure practical reason alone. It needs to encompass the preservation of an "imaginary domain," by which she means "the moral and psychic right to represent and articulate the meaning of our desire and our sexuality within the ethical framework of respect for the dignity of all others." Unlike the feminist approaches that Stoljar describes, Cornell is less interested in whether an agent's current desires are distorted or not and more interested in respecting an agent's capacity, in principle, to "articulate their desire as well as morally evaluate their ends." Cornell sees "the feminine within the imaginary domain" as connected to biology and reproduction but also not reducible to it. The feminist in the imaginary domain also takes up how the laws of culture shape kinship and family structures. It also concerns "the subjective aspect of the assumption of sexual identity—the process through which we internalize both an image and a set of norms that shape who we are as well as who we desire and love."

Cornell is not repudiating the linguistic turn. Rather, by situating her project in a psychoanalytic frame, she sees how the subject who the socio-symbolic attempts to normalize can still resist and transform her world. She points to Butler who "shows us that gender identity is never simply passively internalized as images and static norms. These images and norms are shaped as we externalize them and act out our lives as men and women." We are not merely assuming identities that are foisted on us, we "also live them… We are the ones who externalize the meaning of gender… The more we actively assume our desire, the less we are captured by traditional gender roles. We become able to assume special responsibility for our lives." Instead of seeing desire as potentially heteronomous, she sees it as a resource for becoming truly free, an ally in the project of autonomy.

To most of her readers—students and scholars in the tradition of contemporary continental philosophy—it is strange to see a feminist lauding Enlightenment ideals like autonomy, freedom, and dignity. Cornell argues that these ideals need not be hopelessly individualistic and rationalistic. If read in a psychoanalytic vein they can be wrested free of "a pre-Freudian understanding of desire."

A pre-Freudian theory of desire values only what is conscious and rational. If it knew of the unconscious it would dismiss it as irrational, as truly the Other—but also dismiss its resources for imagining and trying to bring about a world in which one might really be free. What one *really* wants might be deeply buried, just as perhaps the real desires of the deferential wife whose daily conscious life might be a mass of contradictions but her unconscious a source of freedom. As Cornelius Castoriadis, whom Cornell cites, writes, "Autonomy is therefore not a clarification without remainder nor is it the total diminution of the discourse of the Other unrecognized as such. It is the establishment of another relationship between the discourse of the Other and the subject's discourse."

Cornell is providing language for Joel Whitebook's insight that there is in the psyche a constitutional factor that resists conformism. By projecting ourselves as free, Cornell writes, we can "claim our person: it helps us distinguish between entrapment in an imaginary configuration and the imaginative labor of our own radical imagination." As for feminist theorists who want to weigh in on whether or not a woman's desires are really her own, Cornell concludes, "A feminism that insists on the psychic entitlement as well as the legal right of all women to claim their own person—and with their person, their desire—will be reluctant to label as false consciousness women's attempts to pursue this goal." Where some earlier feminists sought to police the bounds of what a woman should want, to make sure they didn't become "deferential housewives," Cornell is calling for a feminism that sees women "re-inventing and transforming" the meaning of their own desire.

> There is no such thing as authentic desire that is absolutely true to feminist aspirations. There is no bright line between good desires and bad desires because the whole point

here is to emphasize the importance of women claiming their desiring subjectivity. In the name of dignity and its translation into the ideal of the person, we should keep the psychic space open for women to begin to act out their desires, to see what happens and how they will change.

Where other feminist theories focused on the content of the desire itself, Cornell is focusing on the dignity of the subject herself and holding out a space for that subject to create new visions of what a good life will be.

Chapter 6
Feminist Ways of Living

Introduction

For all the complicated philosophical questions that feminism raises, ultimately it is a political movement that aims to change the social and political institutions and practices that have harmed women for millennia. It has been a movement for women's liberation: liberation from all the forms of oppression we surveyed in chapter three, which are undergirded by the ways of thinking considered in chapter four. As a political movement, feminists have brought this struggle for liberation to many venues. In the winter of 1917, women held vigil in Lafayette Park, across from the United States White House, calling for the right to vote. In the 1960s, women's living rooms became spaces for consciousness raising. In the late twentieth century, women took to the courts to demand equal rights, one champion being "the notorious" Ruth Bader Ginsburg. Today women are fighting in legislatures throughout the United States that are stripping women of the right to an abortion. In the United Nations, feminists have been involved in campaigns to fight climate change, since much climate change inordinately affects women and children, especially in the developing world. In these various arenas they have taken up a host of issues including matters of sexual violence against women, reproductive freedom, job discrimination, and sexual harassment.

On many political issues feminists agree. For the most part, feminists agree that rape and other forms of violence and harassment against women should be criminalized. They agree that women should have freedom to make their own reproductive choices. And they agree that the persistence of discrimination against women in the workplace should end.

But while there is agreement on these issues, feminists often agree for different reasons. For example, there is universal feminist agreement that rape is wrong, but a wide array of reasons about what makes it wrong. Is it all about violence, or power, or lust? What counts for consent? Is it a crime against the person or a crime against humanity?

And on other political issues, feminists have taken diametrically opposed positions, most notably on pornography and sex work, with some feminists arguing that these are prima facie wrong and others seeing them as possible choices that women might freely engage in.

To understand how and why feminists take different political stances, it helps to see the variety of political and philosophical positions that are at work within feminism itself. So let me lay out what these various schools of thought are in feminism. I will focus on a representative sample of approaches and touch on how these approach various political issues of concern to women.

Liberal Feminism

Liberal feminism may be the most familiar. The word *liberal* harkens back to John Locke's seventeenth century theory on the civil liberties that all men (and yes, just men) have even in the state of nature, prior to the establishment of government. (This is known as classical liberalism.) These "inalienable" rights made their way into the constitutions of most modern, liberal nation states: freedom, equality, property, or happiness. As inalienable, these were taken to be rights that no state could infringe. In the twentieth century, one strand of classical liberalism became libertarianism, a view that the state should keep its hands off people's private affairs, especially their right to property. Another strand of classical liberalism became what we think of today as liberal more broadly, as a contrast to conservative politics. This kind of contemporary liberalism sees a role for the state in ensuring that people are treated freely and equally.

All these varieties of liberalism generally hold to a distinction between state and society, or the public and the private realms; that is, a distinction between the government (public) and the people (private). The private realm includes both households and the "private sector" of businesses and markets. Generally, libertarians believe that households and the private sector should be as free from governmental regulation as possible. Contemporary liberal theorists are open to regulating the private sphere, at least when there is a compelling state interest to do so. A major part of their justification for this flows from their use of the work of John Rawls, a late twentieth century liberal theorist who developed an account of the principles of a just society. His "ideal theory" starts with this vision of a just society and what elements it should contain. Critics of ideal theory argue for "non-ideal theory" which would begin with the world's imperfections— including gender injustice—and focus on the work that needs to be done to ameliorate these. Charles Mills puts the distinction thus: "[W]hat distinguishes ideal theory is not merely the *use* of ideals, since obviously non ideal theory can and will use ideals also (certainly it will appeal to the moral ideals, if it may be more dubious about the value of invoking idealized human capacities). What distinguishes ideal theory is the reliance on idealization to the exclusion, or at least marginalization, of the actual." As a liberal theory, liberal feminism is most susceptible to falling into the trap of idealizing the just society and not focusing sufficiently on messy realities. Most of the other feminist philosophies we will turn to are very much in the non-ideal theory vein.

Liberal theory also tends to take the main unit of analysis as the individual. Feminist theorists have long criticized liberalism's—including liberal feminism's—tendency to overlook the social and kinship bonds that tie people together and the ways that people are nurtured and raised through others' care. To this criticism, Martha Nussbaum replies these forms of care work are part of women's oppression, not a starting point for a feminist theory. "Women have all too often been regarded not as ends but as means to the ends of others, not as sources of agency and worth in their own right but as reproducers and caregivers." Liberalism offers women more, she argues, namely an "insistence on the separateness of one life from another, and the equal importance of each life." Liberalism "insists that the goal of politics should be the amelioration of lives taken one by one as separate ends, rather than the amelioration of the organic whole or the totality." To those who worry that liberalism might fail to provide people with what they need to flourish in the world, Nussbaum's answer is that society should take care to tend to people's capabilities. Her capabilities' approach calls for a robust role for the social order to ensure people's capacities are cultivated.

With a few exceptions, liberal feminists agree that there is often a need for public action to protect women's freedom and equality. They base their positions on a rich conception of civil liberties. And unlike John Locke who very much meant "men," not *all* people, when he laid out his theory, liberal feminists have worked to ferret out spaces in which women have been denied the protections that men have, whether under the law or in unfettered commercial and market practices. They have also helped chip away at the wall separating the public from the private, saying there is a space for the law to protect women in their homes rather than leaving the household as the husband's little kingdom. Liberal feminists helped bring women their own checkbook, the right to charge their husbands with rape, the grounds for filing complaints of sexual harassment and unequal treatment in the workplace.

Socialist and Marxist Feminisms

As feminist thought developed into the 1970s and 1980s, feminist political philosophy became more entwined with conventional political philosophies, most of which at that time were focused on systems of national governance and the kinds of economic systems they favored. There were liberal philosophers who took capitalism for granted and Marxist and socialist philosophers who found capitalism to be largely a source of suffering. Those who worked out of a socialist and Marxist orientation focused largely on either the redistribution of income (socialist) or the ownership of the means of production (Marxist). Feminists theorists working in these traditions likewise tried to understand women's subordination through an economic lens, with socialist feminists arguing for, among other things, women's labor in the home being renumerated and Marxist feminists, such as Angela Davis, interpreting gender divisions as a species of class divisions.

The end of the Cold War brought a major shift in political philosophy, when political change happened through public action on the streets of Berlin and Prague and not through any direct intervention in forms of governance. With this shift, political philosophers, feminists included, began focusing more on the public sphere. Soon there were fewer avowedly Marxist political philosophers and more "critical theorists." Critical theory is a strain of thought dating back to the 1930s in Germany when social theorists began to use the social sciences to understand why Marx's predictions failed to come through. They suspected that the problems with capitalism could not be reduced to class antagonism, and so turned their attention to deeper issues concerning the nature of consciousness and forms of social domination and control that are not directly economic. However, some critical theories still worry about social and economic justice, for example, Nancy Fraser has continued to argue for the need for economic redistribution.

Many feminists who are not explicitly socialist or Marxist feminists are still concerned about economic and social precarity in the "neoliberal" turn that contemporary politics has taken. These feminist critics are worried about how neoliberalism demands resiliency in the face of increasing precarity. We can see this in the work of Judith Butler, Wendy Brown, and Albena Azmanova, among others. Butler borrows from Michel Foucault's late work on biopolitics, examining how neoliberal demands for autonomy, self-sufficiency, self-discipline, and self-investment impact individuals on the level of subjectivity, making both life and the possibility of political action to transform the conditions of life increasingly untenable. Individuals, they argue, are met with increasing vulnerability to economic forces and fewer resources to overcome vulnerability due to social isolation and limited access to social services. Some feminists study how subjectivity, affect, and morality accommodate these neoliberal trends. For instance, this shows up in how the demand to "overcome vulnerability" via the contemporary emphasis on individual "resilience" attempts to transform vulnerable persons, especially women, into productive neoliberal subjects. Instead, many feminist critiques challenge neoliberal individualism by reasserting that agency need not be synonymous with autonomy, and propose non-sovereign or relational accounts of the agentic subject instead.

Radical Feminism

A second group I'll turn to is one that calls itself "radical feminism." The word *radical* is meant in the mathematical sense of getting to the root of a problem, and what they find at the root of the problem of sexism and all forms of oppression is the domination of women. It's not that there is a mistake about women's nature, a confusion about gender, or an erroneous view about who has dignity and inalienable rights and who does not. It is that, as MacKinnon said (see chapter four), on day one man dominated women.

"Sex class is so deep as to be invisible," writes Shulamith Firestone in her manifesto for radical feminism, *The Dialectic of Sex*. Her term "sex class" refers to the way sex is always framed by domination of men over women, just as Marx and Engels saw workers dominated by capitalists. But sex class is much more primordial than economic classes. It is so deeply entrenched in our culture—and frames everything about our culture—that we don't see it as a matter of domination but just as "natural" divisions. For millennia, there was little women could do about this, Firestone argues, because women really were tied down by biological exigencies from menstruation to childbearing. But now, as she writes, in 1970, technologies like the pill are making it possible for women to have better lives. Ultimately, technology should allow women to break out of sex class domination altogether.

Radical feminism grew out of the cultural and artistic women's movements of the 1960s. From its beginnings, it was focused on creating spaces for women, eschewing men from participation in their events all the way down to changing the word "women" to "womyn," among other variations. The radical feminist Mary Daly for years prevented men from taking her classes at Boston College. From 1976 to 2015, the Michigan Womyn's Music Festival admitted only those born female, excluding all men and all transwomen. Today, a subset of radical feminists known as TERFS or Trans Exclusionary Radical Feminists, oppose considering transwomen as women.

Radical feminism can be unflinching in its pronouncements and denouncements, more theoretically direct than sophisticated. A prime example is the late Andrea Dworkin, who likened heterosexual sex as equivalent to raping women and pornography as a matter of men possessing women. In general, radical feminists include "feminists who stress essential or very deep rooted differences between men and women, and who celebrate the distinctive modes of embodiment and experiential capacities that women have," writes Kathleen Lennon. Radical feminists have been "centrally involved in highlighting sexual violence against women globally, which they sometimes see as rooted in male nature, or deep processes of socialization."

Care Ethics

About twenty-three hundred years after Aristotle argued that men had better moral judgment than women, a Harvard social psychologist by the name of Lawrence Kohlberg conducted a study that would affirm Aristotle's view. The study was a series of interviews with boys and girls from elementary school through the cusp of adulthood, posing to them a hypothetical conundrum: A man named Heinz had a wife on her deathbed. There was one drug that could save her, but Heinz had only half of what the one druggist who had the drug was charging. Heinz begged the druggist for help, but the druggist refused. So that night Heinz broke in to the laboratory and stole the drug. The question put to the children in the study was this: Should Heinz have stolen the drug? Why or why not?

Kohlberg and his research assistants recorded the children's answers and noted whether the responses were based on matters of principle (such as "it is wrong to steal" or "profits over sickness are wrong") or conventional social expectations (such as care for a loved one or conformity to social expectations). The researchers were less interested in whether the respondents thought Heinz was right or wrong but *why* they thought he was right or wrong. Drawing on previous social psychological and philosophical theories, Kohlberg grouped the answers from least morally developed (pre-conventional, such as worries about being punished) to conventional (love and care for one's fellows and community norms) to the most developed, post-conventional reasons based on abstract principles that should apply universally. The idea was that, while a child might be motivated by the expectations and norms of one's culture, a more developed thinker would be able to transcend those conventional expectations and ascertain what was universally correct. Instead of saying the druggist should have cared about the man's wife, for example, a more morally developed child would say that one should be concerned about the health of all, including the wife's. Then care for the wife wouldn't be a particular, conventional response, but one based on an abstract principle.

As the researchers began tabulating the results, one result was striking: boys seemed to be developing morally faster than girls, and some girls never caught up. This struck one of the research assistants as suspicious. And in 1975 she sat down at her kitchen table to write a book about her worries, a book that would make her, Carol Gilligan, internationally famous. *In A Different Voice* argued that girls' responses were not less developed but rather that Kohlberg's scale had a masculinist bias. Who is to say that it is "more" developed to address the Heinz dilemma from principle rather than care? Who is to say that concern about particular relationships, community, and kinship matters less than universal principles? Gilligan argued that the girls' responses were not less than boys', they were different than boys'.

Out of Gilligan's and other kindred work, a new feminist philosophical approach emerged: care ethics, which argues that care for particular others is just as legitimate and worthy as concern for abstract principles. In philosophical language, these approaches can be shortened to "the good" and "the right," with the former being attentive to what is good for a particular community and the latter concerned with the principles that will lead to a just society. Drawing on feminist research in moral psychology, care ethics explores the ways in which the good, here the virtues that society and mothering cultivate in women, can provide an alternative to the traditional emphases in moral and political philosophy on the right, that is, universality, reason, and justice. Some care ethicists have sought to take the virtues that had long been relegated to the private realm, such as paying particular attention to those who are vulnerable or taking into consideration circumstances and not just abstract principles, and use them in the public realm as well.

This approach has led to intense debates between liberals who advocated universal ideals of justice and care ethicists who advocated attention to the particular, to relationships, to care. By the 1990s, however, many care ethicists had revised their views. Rather than seeing care and justice as mutually exclusive alternatives, they began to recognize that attention to care should be accompanied by attention to fairness (justice) in order to attend to the plight of those with whom we have no immediate relation.

At the same time that Gilligan was publishing her early work, the political philosopher John Rawls was publishing his *Theory of Justice*, which was all about divining the appropriate principles that would lead to a just society.

Many political philosophers – including liberal feminist philosophers — followed Rawls' lead, looking for principled ways to create a more just society. But another camp of political philosophy emerged in contrast, "communitarians," philosophers and social theorists who worried about the individualist bent of Rawls' theory and wanted to focus on developing stronger relationships and commitment to the common good (and hear in that the other side of the "just versus the good" dichotomy.) Likewise, many feminist thinkers were taken by Gilligan's worries about the individualism of Kohlberg's approach. Some of those feminist thinkers highlighted the long neglected virtues of motherhood, the need to valorize maternalism. These "maternalist" feminists pointed out how the human race would never have flourished were it not for mothers and that we need to value love and care as much, if not more, than individualism and justice. As Virginia Held put it, for too long philosophers have treated people as if they were mushrooms who popped up fully developed, when it was women, mothers, who nurtured people into their adulthood.

To return to our discussion of metaphysical imaginaries, note that what is at issue in these debates is the binary of reason/emotion, a binary that has long been hierarchical, valorizing reason over emotion. Feminist care ethicists and maternalists want to flip the binary, or at least in some way refuse to grant any priority of reason over emotion. But they leave the binary in place.

Also note that care ethicists and maternalists take for granted that women have greater capacity for care and nurturing than men, or maybe they mean more of a proclivity. It is not really clear. In any case they are not taking issue with the way that women—and not men—are gendered to care for others. They even suggest that women have a more natural capacity for care. This is a quite problematic view.

The care ethics approach raises the question of whether and, if so, how women-as-care-givers have distinct virtues. Feminists as a whole have long distanced themselves from the idea that women have any particular essence, choosing instead to see femininity and its accompanying virtues as social constructs, dispositions that result from culture and conditioning, certainly not biological givens. So for care ethicists to champion the virtues that have inculcated femininity seems also to champion a patriarchal system that relegates one gender to the role of caretaker.

The care ethicists' answer to this problem has largely been to flip the hierarchy, to claim that the work of the household is more meaningful and sustaining than the work of the polis. But critics, such as Drucilla Cornell, Mary Dietz, and Chantal Mouffe, argue that such a revaluation keeps intact the dichotomy between the private and the public and the old association of women's work with childcare.

Disregard for the role of emotion in political life has long been a policy in the history of philosophy, in particular because emotionality—like care—is frequently associated with women and racialized others. However, women philosophers have insisted on the importance of this intersection. Building on the contributions of feminist care ethicists and difference feminists who worked to show the significance of positive affects typically associated with femininity—such as love, interest, and care—in ethical encounters; other thinkers worried that this appraisal merely reified a false (gendered) dichotomy between reason and emotion, mind and body. Instead, early work by Alison Jaggar, Elizabeth Spelman, Genevieve Lloyd, Elizabeth Grosz, and others argued that reason is both embodied and emotion-laden, and that emotion is an important resource for epistemology in particular. Building on this work, feminist political theorists have argued that understanding the role of emotion and affect is crucial for understanding a number of important political phenomena: motivation for action, collective action and community formation, solidarity and patriotism, as well as vulnerability, racism and xenophobia. Meanwhile, others examine the political significance of specific emotions, for instance: shame, precarity and grief, anger, fear, and love.

Democratic Feminisms

As Mary Dietz writes in her 2003 essay on current controversies in feminist theory, "In recent years, political theorists have been engaged in debates about what it might mean to conceptualize a feminist political praxis that is aligned with democracy but does not begin from the binary of gender." The constellation of thinkers engaged in this project are working in what we could call performative political philosophy. This political philosophy is performative in several senses: in theorizing how agency is constituted, how political judgments can be made in the absence of known rules, how new universals can be created and new communities constituted. Performative politics doesn't worry about whether it is possible to come up with a single definition of "woman" or any other political identity; it sees identity as something that is performatively created. Performative feminism can be understood, in the words of Linda Zerilli, as a call for a "freedom-centered feminism" that "would strive to bring about transformation in normative conceptions of gender without returning to the classical notion of freedom as sovereignty" that feminists have long criticized but found difficult to resist.

From a performative feminist perspective, feminism is a project of anticipating and creating better political futures in the absence of foundations. Taking its cue from Judith Butler's performative account of gender as well as Hannah Arendt's observation that human rights are created politically, performative feminism describes an anticipatory ideal of politics, which Zerilli characterizes as "the contingently based public practice of soliciting the agreement of others to what each of us claims to be universal." This view recuperates many of the ideals of the Enlightenment—such as freedom, autonomy, and justice—but in a way that drops their grounding in metaphysical assumptions about reason, progress, and human nature. Instead, this new view sees them as ideals that people hold and try to instantiate through practice and imagination. Normative political claims appeal to other people. For example, even if there is no metaphysical truth that human beings have dignity and infinite worth, people can act as if it were true in order to create a world in which it is seen to be so. Even as performative feminist political philosophy shares liberal feminism's appreciation for Enlightenment ideals, it does so in a way that is skeptical about foundations.

Despite the shared post-foundational theorizing among performative feminists, there are sharp divergences on the question of, as Dietz puts it, "what it means to actualize public spaces and enact democratic politics." On this question, theorists tend to split into two groups: associational and agonistic. Associational theorists gravitate more toward deliberative democratic theory, while agonistic theorists worry that democratic theories that focus on consensus can silence debate and thus they focus more on plurality, dissensus, and the ceaseless contestation within politics.

Associational theorists tend to look for ways, amidst all the differences and questions about the lack of foundations, it is possible to come to agreement on matters of common concern. This is seen in feminist democratic theory, perhaps best known through the works of Seyla Benhabib. Following the democratic theorist Jürgen Habermas, she takes the sign of political legitimacy to be a state of affairs to which all affected would assent. In order for members of a political community to arrive at democratic outcomes, however, the proceedings need to be deliberative. Some associational theorists take deliberation to be a matter of reasoned argumentation; others see it as less about reason or argumentation but more about an open process of working through choices.

Not all theorists who tend toward the associational model embrace deliberative theory so readily. Where Benhabib is confident that conditions can be such that all who are affected can have a voice in deliberations, critics such as Iris Young point out that those who have been historically silenced have a difficult time having their views heard or heeded and are skeptical of the claim that democratic deliberative processes could lead to outcomes that would be acceptable to all. Young worries that deliberation as defined by Habermas is too reason-based and leaves out forms of communication that women and people of color tend to use, including, as she puts it, "greeting, rhetoric, and storytelling." Instead, she proposes a theory of communicative democracy, hoping to make way for a deliberative conception open to means of expression beyond the rational expression of mainstream deliberative democratic theory.

Where liberal feminists and democratic feminists hold out the hope that democratic deliberations might lead to democratic agreements, agonistic feminists are wary of consensus as inherently undemocratic. Their central claim is that feminist struggle, like other struggles for social justice, is engaged in politics as ceaseless contestation: politics are inherently conflictual, and battles over power and hegemony are the central tasks of democratic struggle. They worry that consensus sought by democratic theorists will lead to oppression or injustice by silencing new struggles. As Chantal Mouffe writes, "We have to accept that every consensus exists as a temporary result of a provisional hegemony, as a stabilization of power, and that it always entails some form of exclusion." Where associational theorists seek out ways that people can overcome systematically distorted communication and deliberation, Dietz notes that agonists eschew this project, instead, "deconstruct[ing] emancipatory procedures to disclose how the subject is both produced through political exclusions and positioned against them."

New work in democratic theory offers hope of moving beyond the associational/agonistic divide in performative feminist politics. Benhabib's proceduralism is being surpassed with more affect-laden accounts of deliberation. Instead of the rational back-and-forth of reasoned argumentation, theorists are beginning to see deliberative talk as forms of constituting the subject, judging without pre-conceived truths, and performatively creating new political projects.

Transcontinental Feminisms

We saw in earlier chapters how historically there has been a tension running throughout feminist theory and practice about who the subject of feminism is, mainly the tendency for white middle class feminists to paint a picture of what women are in their own image. This has been true in Anglo-American feminisms as well as in Continental feminism, especially with "the continent" presumed to be Europe. To be fair, some of the resources that feminism found in Europe of the late twentieth century paved the way for moving beyond this. Those resources included Michel Foucault's critique of the construction of subjectivity, the phenomenologists' attention to embodiment, Jacques Derrida's critique of totalizing presumptions about language, much of the linguistic turn described in chapter five, and psychoanalytic insights into how human beings are largely strangers to themselves. All these movements helped decenter older notions about the autonomous sovereign (read, male) subject, including the old "man of reason."

In the past two decades, feminists working within these various continental traditions have gone further. As the authors of the entry on continental feminism in the *Stanford Encyclopedia of Philosophy* write,

> While all feminist theorizing deals with questions of power, subjectivity, and culture, Continental feminist approaches

to these issues are often *critical* in the sense that they explore how external power dynamics affect the constitution of inner experiences, and in turn how embodied and subjective re-articulations of power can and should transform the world in the pursuit of justice. This frequently involves taking lived experience as a crucial component of critical philosophy.

With their attention to lived experience, a new generation is calling itself "transContinental feminism." The authors of the SEP entry quote Kyoo Lee and Alyson Cole, who write that "'trans' serves as a marker for the constant geo-cultural flows of ideas in transit, as in 'transatlantic', 'transpacific', 'transoceanic', etc., as well as for cutting-edge works, conversations, and debates in trans-critical, cultural, disciplinary, human, gender, genic, lingual, medial, national fields, etc., and as trans*feminist discourses."

Under this heading, there is an immense amount of work going on race and ethnicity. People at the intersection of multiple marginalized identities (e.g, Black women) have raised questions about which identity is foremost or whether either identity is apt. Such questions play out with the question of political representation. Anne Phillips and Iris Young have each asked what aspects of identity are politically salient and truly representative, whether race, class, or gender. The ontological question of women's identity gets played out on the political stage when it comes to matters of political representation, group rights, and affirmative action. The 2008 U.S. Democratic Party primary battle between Senators Barack Obama and Hillary Clinton turned this philosophical question into a very real and heated one from Black women throughout the United States. Was a Black woman who supported Clinton a traitor to her race, or a Black woman who supported Obama a traitor to her sex? Or did it make any sense to talk about identity in a way that would lead to charges of treason?

In the 1980s and 1990s, philosophy, along with the rest of Western culture, started responding to demands for multicultural and non-European perspectives. Over the past few decades, contemporary continental feminism, with its interest in questions of identity and representation, has been influenced by multicultural, post-colonial, and now decolonial theory. Moreover, the demographics of continental feminist philosophy have broadened to include people of color and those from beyond the European-American orbit.

By the late 1980s, postcolonial theory raised the need to become aware of multiple global perspectives. As Sharon Krause describes it, "this development involved the 'world diversification' of feminism to a more global, comparative, and differentiated body of work." This diversification, Krause notes, is also due to new literature on intersectionality, that is, the ways in which the intersections of our multiple identities (race, gender, orientation, ethnicity, etc.) all need to be attended to in talking about political change. "The result," Krause writes, "is an explosion of knowledge about the lived experience of differently placed and multiply-positioned women."

Decolonial feminists overlap in many areas with other women of color feminists, but they bring several unique concerns specific to the colonial and post-colonial experience. In contemporary decolonial theory, these concerns are largely framed within the discourse of "coloniality," first theorized in terms of "coloniality of power" by Aníbal Quijano. Here, "coloniality" refers to how relations between colonizer and colonized, such as relations of labor, subjectivity, and authority, are racialized around the colonial system of capitalist exploitation. For decolonial feminist thinkers, gender is another axis around which the global capitalist system of power classifies and dehumanizes people, a colonial imposition in tension with non-modern cosmologies, economies, and modes of kinship. Echoing Quijano, María Lugones calls this the "coloniality of gender," noting that de-colonizing gender is part of a wider project of decolonial resistance opposed to the categorial, dichotomous, and hierarchical logics of capitalist modernity that are rooted in the colonization of the Americas.

This movement we call feminism arose in the context of societies' self-understanding as democratic. While many feminists still see their nemesis as patriarchy, it is in fact not that but a supposedly democratic fraternal order. As we have seen, the term *patriarchy* is a poor catchall term to explain the condition that women find themselves in of late. It might be of use during times when societies have been ruled by clan leaders, but it does not help understand the seemingly bizarre hypocrisy of women being denied equal treatment in a democracy. One would think that the Enlightenment ideal of equality for all would extend to those otherwise marginalized and oppressed. But oddly women's situation can be just as bad in a democracy.

Feminist theory tries to make sense of this. It begins with attention to women, to their roles and locations. It considers how women as a group are situated as well as the great variety of women's concerns that makes it difficult to pin down what it is to be a woman. New work that troubles the gender binary has made this matter even more complex. Nonetheless, feminist theory takes up the complexities of a woman's situatedness, including her class, race, ability, and sexuality. And in so doing, feminist theory scrutinizes the way that conventional theorizing undervalues or ignores women's experience.

One element it attends to is the specific ways in which women are oppressed. This is not a cookie-cutter problem. Oppression has many faces, and not

Closing Thoughts

all the faces affect every oppressed group though they do impact a variety of groups—poor people, old people, people of color, women, indigenous people, LGBTQ people. But not in the same way. A low-income geriatric white man may face powerlessness, but less likely violence. A transman may daily fear violence but perhaps not embodied oppression. For the sake of our topic, feminism, I think it is safe to say that women face many of these forms of oppression, especially as they age. And women of color experience just about all of them all the time.

As we've seen, the fault does not lie with particular actors' bad intentions. The roots are larger: exploitation arises out of broad economic structures; marginalization also emerges from historical prejudices about who is of value socially and economically and who is not; powerlessness emerges out of inequities in access to social and professional "respectability"; violence grows out of deeply entrenched notions about who is free to be in the world and who should be in constant fear and terror; and embodied oppression grows from human vulnerability to toxic environments and the differential ways that people are situated in them.

Moreover, oppression is not random; it is structural. It operates according to a logic that has already divided the world between those who are worthy and those who are dispensable. And in its incessant operation it reinforces and perpetuates these divisions. A woman afraid to walk alone at night is less likely to do so. A person seemingly unqualified for a job will be less likely to try. Those who do not look like the mainstream are less likely to enter it. Those who have been made sick by a culture are less likely to thrive. Oppression is not accidental, it is systemic and intentional, even if all those involved in it are largely unaware.

We have also now seen what upholds these structures: the deep psychological and often unconscious ways of seeing the world, what I call the ruling imaginaries, the metaphysics of sex. As we've seen, it is no accident that the term "man" parades as standing for all of humanity when in fact being exclusively meant for men alone. Moreover, the ideal of man/human is based on a series of hierarchical binaries that privilege reason over passion, mind over body, and culture over nature, all the while assigning the feminine to the negative pole. Furthermore, women are trapped in a riddle of being creatures whose essence is mere matter, but matter has no essence. And all this comes back to metaphysical notions of what an ideal person is, conveniently connected to what a young strong male body is in the height of its lust: strong, stiff, direct, and penetrating. It's a wonder that there is any woman at all.

Feminism began with a call for women's freedom, and by the end of the twentieth century it had to circle back to thinking through what freedom could even mean. The linguistic turn seemed to spell the end of agency for individuals and communities to resist the normalizing power of the socio-symbolic realm. Freud's discovery of the unconscious could have made things only worse, but in it there was a kernel for resistance, a "constitutional factor," perhaps one's temperament, perhaps desire itself. This is good news for feminism: Instead of policing women's desires, psychoanalysis opens the door for people to imagine and create new worlds.

On the question of how we should live, feminists have developed a huge array of responses. While they share some of what Gerda Lerner identified as aspects of feminist consciousness, particularly "the awareness of women that they belong to a subordinate group and that, as members of such a group, they have suffered wrongs," "the recognition that their condition of subordination is not natural, but societally determined" and the need for developing "an alternate vision of the future," they disagree on particular solutions. Still there is a shared commitment to transforming and overturning the kinds of practices that have for millennia diminished women's lives.

Having read this quick immersion, perhaps the reader will come away with both a better understanding of the varieties of feminist thought and concerns and a surer sense of what her own feminist orientation might be. Radical, to get to the heart of the matter? Liberal, to make sure people's fundamental rights are preserved? Socialist, to attend to the consequences of neoliberal globalization? Democratic, to find a better way for all of us to live together? Or maybe care oriented, to make space for cherishing the important work that women have done through all of human history. And also transcontinental, to take in perspectives from beyond the European-American frame. Perhaps the reader, like this author, will be torn, finding something of value in all these perspectives.

Likely, too, the reader may be more worried than before picking up this book at how daunting it is to counter the ancient history of patriarchy and its more recent takeover by a fraternal order. So much of what we are taught to believe is natural, is "just the way things are," is a construct designed to diminish, or really, oppress women. To be a feminist is to be attuned to these phenomena and to be creative in finding ways to move forward. And, as Sara Ahmed writes, it is to be someone who stands up, speaks back, and risks lives, homes, and relationships "in the struggle for more bearable worlds."

Further Reading

Alcoff, Linda. (Ed.) (2003) *Singing in the Fire: Stories of Women in Philosophy*. Rowman & Littlefield.

Ahmed, Sara (2017). *Living a Feminist Life*, Durham, NC: Duke University Press Books.

Allen, Amy (2008). *The Politics of Our Selves: Power, Autonomy, and Gender in Contemporary Critical Theory*, New York: Columbia University Press.

Anzaldúa, Gloria (1987). *Borderlands/la frontera: The New Mestiza*, San Francisco, CA: Spinsters/Aunt Lute.

Azmanova, Albena (2020). *Capitalism on Edge*. New York: Columbia University Press.

Bachofen, Johann Jakob (2003). *An English Translation of Bachofen's Mutterrecht* (Mother Right) (abridged) (1861). trans. David Partenheimer. The Edwin Mellen Press.

Beauvoir, Simone de (1952). *The Second Sex*. New York: Vintage Books.

Bettcher, Talia Mae (2018). "'When Tables Speak': On the Existence of Trans Philosophy*," *Daily Nous*, May 30, 2018. URL = *https://dailynous.com/2018/05/30/tables-speak-existence-trans-philosophy-guest-talia-mae-bettcher/*

Butler, Judith (1990). *Gender Trouble: Feminism and the Subversion of Identity*, New York: Routledge.

Butler, Judith (2004). *Precarious Life: The Powers of Mourning and Violence*, New York: Verso.

Brown, Wendy (2015). *Undoing the Demos: Neoliberalism's Stealth Revolution*. Zone Books.

Chanter, Tina (ed.) (2009). *Rethinking Sex and Gender*, Cambridge: Cambridge University Press.

Collins, Patricia Hill (1990). *Black Feminist Thought*, Boston, MA: Unwin Hyman, 1990.

Cornell, Drucilla (2003). "Autonomy Re-Imagined," *JPCS: Journal for the Psychoanalysis of Culture & Society*, Volume 8, Number 1, Spring 2003.

Cixous, Hélène (1986). "Sorties: Out and Out: Attacks/Ways Out/Forays, *The Newly Born Woman*, trans. by Betsy Wing. Minneapolis: University of Minnesota Press.

Davis, Angela (1983). *Women, Race & Class.* Vintage Books.

Diaz-Leon, Esa (2016). "'Woman' as a Politically Significant Term: A Solution to the Puzzle," *Hypatia: A Journal of Feminist Philosophy* 31:2 (2016): 245-256.

Dietz, Mary (2003). "Current controversies in feminist theory," *Annual Review of Political Science*, 6: 399–431.

Eller, Cynthia (2000). *The Myth of Matriarchal Prehistory.* Boston: Beacon Press.

Firestone, Shulamith (1970). *The Dialectic of Sex: The Case for Feminist Revolution*, New York: Bantam.

Freud, Sigmund, James Strachey, Anna Freud, and Angela Richards (1966). *The Standard edition of the complete psychological works of Sigmund Freud.* London: Hogarth Press.

Fuss, Diana (1989). *Essentially Speaking: Feminism, Nature & Difference.* New York and London: Routledge.

Garry, Ann, Serene J. Khader, and Alison Stone (2017). *The Routledge Companion to Feminist Philosophy.* New York and London: Routledge.

Haslanger, Sally (2012). *Resisting Reality: Social Construction and Social Critique*. Oxford: Oxford University Press.

Honig, Bonnie (2001). *Democracy and the Foreigner*. Princeton: Princeton University Press.

Huseyinzadegan, Dilek, Jana McAuliffe, Jameliah Inga Shorter-Bourhanou, B. Tamsin Kimoto, Ege Selin Islekel, Marie Draz, and Erika Brown, "Continental Feminism", *The Stanford Encyclopedia of Philosophy* (Winter 2020 Edition), Edward N. Zalta (ed.), URL = <*https://plato.stanford.edu/archives/win2020/entries/femapproach-continental/*>.

Held, Virginia (2007). *The Ethics of Care: Personal, Political, and Global*. Oxford: Oxford University Press.

Irigaray, Luce (1985). *This Sex Which is Not One*. Ithaca, NY: Cornell University Press.

Jaggar, Alison M. (1983). *Feminist Politics and Human Nature*, Lanham, MD: Rowman and Littlefield.

Lennon, Kathleen, "Feminist Perspectives on the Body." *The Stanford Encyclopedia of Philosophy* (Fall 2019 Edition), Edward N. Zalta (ed.), URL = <*https://plato.stanford.edu/archives/fall2019/entries/feminist-body/*>.

Lerner, Gerda (1986). *The Creation of Patriarchy.* Oxford: Oxford University Press.

Mann, B., McKenna, E., Russell, C., & Zambrana, R. (2019). The Promise of Feminist Philosophy. *Hypatia, 34*(3), 394-400. doi:10.1111/hypa.12490.

Mansbridge, Jane (1983). *Beyond Adversary Democracy.* Chicago: University of Chicago Press.

McAfee, Noëlle, "Feminist Philosophy," *The Stanford Encyclopedia of Philosophy* (Fall 2018 Edition), Edward N. Zalta (ed.), URL = <*https://plato.stanford.edu/archives/fall2018/entries/feminist-philosophy/*>. (This entry provides an overview of all of *The Stanford Encyclopedia of Philosophy's* entries on feminist philosophy.)

Mills, Charles (2005). "'Ideal Theory' as Ideology," *Hypatia* Vol. 20, No. 3 (Summer, 2005), pp. 165-184.

Mohanty, Chandra Talpade (1984). "Under Western Eyes: Feminist Scholarship and Colonial Discourses," *boundary 2,* 12(3): 333–358. doi:10.2307/302821

Mohanty, Chandra Talpade (2003). "'Under Western Eyes' Revisited: Feminist Solidarity through Anticapitalist Struggles", *Signs: Journal of Women in Culture and Society*, 28(2): 499–535. doi:10.1086/342914

Nussbaum, Martha C. (1999). *Sex and Social Justice.* New York: Oxford University Press.

Olkowski, Dorothea (2000). "Body, Knowledge and Becoming-Woman: Morpho-logic in Deleuze and Irigaray," *Deleuze and Feminist Theory*, eds. Ian Buchanan and Claire Colebrook, Edinburgh University Press.

Paul, R.A. (2010). "Yes, the Primal Crime Did Take Place: A Further Defense of Freud's *Totem and Taboo*." Ethos, 38: 230-249. *https://doi.org/10.1111/j.1548-1352.2010.01137.x*

Pateman, Carole (1988). *The Sexual Contract.* Cambridge: Polity.

Rawlinson, Mary (2020).*The Betrayal of Substance: Death, Literature, and Sexual Difference in Hegel's "Phenomenology of Spirit."* New York: Columbia University Press.

Ruti, Mari (2020). *Penis Envy & Other Bad Feelings: The Emotional Costs of Everyday Life*. New York: Columbia University Press.

Sheth, Falguni A. (2019). "The Production of Acceptable Muslim Women in the United States," *The Journal of Aesthetics and Art Criticism*, 77: 411-422. *https://doi.org/10.1111/jaac.12667*

Sullivan, Shannon (2015). *The Physiology of Sexist and Racist Oppression*. Oxford University Press.

Watson, Lori. "The Woman Question," *Transgender Studies Quarterly* 3:1-2 (2016): 248-255.

Weiss, Gail, Ann V, Murphy, and Gayle Salamon (2020). *50 Concepts for a Critical Phenomenology*. Northwestern University Press.

Willett, Cynthia. *The Soul of Justice: Social Bonds and Racial Hubris*. Cornell University Press, 2001.

Willett, Cynthia and Julie Willett (2019). *Uproarious: How Feminists and Other Subversive Comics Speak Truth*. Minneapolis: University of Minnesota Press.

Wilson, Elizabeth A. (2015). *Gut Feminism*. Durham: Duke University Press.

World Health Organization (2019). "Violence Against Women." URL = *https://apps.who.int/iris/bitstream/handle/10665/329889/WHO-RHR-19.16-eng.pdf?ua=1*

Young, Iris Marion (1990). *Justice and the Politics of Difference.* Princeton University Press.

Pay a visit to:

Quick Immersion Series

Visit our WEB:
https://www.quickimmersions.com/

You will get:

+Information of all published books

+News of the books in preparation

+You can subscribe to "A Quick Immersion"

+Links to other spaces of our WEB

+Contact us

+Receive timely information on all our titles

www.ingramcontent.com/pod-product-compliance
Lightning Source LLC
LaVergne TN
LVHW051632080426
835511LV00016B/2314